Hugs from the Heart...
Stories by Grand-Moms & Moms

Margaret M. Desjardins

Copyright © Egg Rock Publishing LLC

All rights reserved.

No part of this publication may be reproduced,
stored in a retrieval system, transmitted in any form
or by any means, electronic, mechanical, photocopying,
recording, or otherwise, without prior written
permission of the publisher and author/illustrator.

Published by Egg Rock Publishing LLC
Printed in the U.S.A. by CreateSpace, North Charleston, SC

Hugs from the Heart... Stories by Grand-Moms & Moms
Authored by Margaret M. Desjardins
Layout by Sven M. Dolling

ISBN-13: 978-0692943786 (Custom Universal)
ISBN-10: 0692943781
Library of Congress Control Number:
LCCN: 2017953713
BISAC: Family & Relationships / Parenting / Grandparenting

Copyright © 2018

Hugs from the Heart...

Table of Contents

Preface vii
Acknowledgments viii
The Last Time... x
Poop Talk!... 1
Dancing in the Rain 7
So, What's in a Name? Plenty!... 13
Silence... 21
Lost in a Television 'Time Suck'.. 27
The Butterfly 35
How do You Know when Your Baby is ready to be Born? ...39
The First Day of School:
                Quivering lip?...or Pep in the Step? 47
There's More to Life than Worrying about Germs!! 51
Magic 59
Which House will They/We Pick? 65
And So the Wind Blows 73
My Baby is 14 Months, 15 Days, and 8 Hours Old!............. 77
Kindness... 83
Reflections in the Mirror: I Am My Mom!............................. 87
Quinn 99
Rethinking Toys 103

Favorite Pastimes with the Great-Grandkids 109
The Demise of the Pencil 113
The Makeup Queen.. 119
Moms: Can't Fit into those Size-2 Jeans? 123
The Art of Controlling Drama 129
The Intruder… 135
Let's Go on a Trip: Bring Pop-Pop and Grammy! 145
Your Baby Deserves You… *ALL* of You! 155
Runaway.. 161
Circling the Moon... 165
Grandmother of an Oldest Grandchild…
        Reflections, Past and Present................... 169
Nine Parent Coaching Tips for Battling Math Anxiety 173
The Appointment 179
Parrot Talk: Stressors that Keep You from Seeing 183
The Treasure that Remains... 189
Car Seats – The Best Gift Grandparents Can Receive! 195
Parenting is NOT a 'Judgment-Free Zone' 201
Remember that Dads are Parents Too! 213
Children Teach Us! 219
A Two-Year-Old is like a Blender without a Lid! 225
Hugs from the Heart 234
Contributors 236

Preface

I have always enjoyed storytelling. When I was a little girl, my Mom used to tell me to stop staring at people. What she didn't realize was, that I was, and am, a keen observer of people and things. Like a camera, at the split second that the shutter captures an image, I, too, capture an image or memory—but in my own mind's eye. The ordinary happenings of life as a grandparent have changed the way I look at my world now. The moments are precious, the perspective as a Mimi, so very different from my first time parenting. Being the Mimi has allowed me to watch my grandchildren's world from my own perch, and to watch the job my children have done, all amazing parents, doing the toughest job of all—raising children. Storytelling inspires me to stop, think, and reflect upon the essence of my own moments as a Mom and Mimi—in a way I never realized I could!

Acknowledgments

The road to raising children is never a straight line, but it is in the bends and curves in the road that the greatest family stories emerge. And those stories grow and become more precious as they are repeated over and over at family gatherings, and from generation to generation. The more the road bends, the richer the story-telling! My heartfelt thanks to the Grand-Moms and Moms, who have shared their stories about what it's like to live, and even travel, with little ones. It is a privilege to be able to share your stories in this book, *Hugs from the Heart*. These heart-warming stories will surely bring back memories to all Grand-Moms and Moms out there.

A great big thanks goes out to the following guest authors who wrote these lovely stories—your stories form the heartbeats of this book: Paulette Buco; Tricia Murphy Duffy; Jan McGregor; Amy Ruocco; Lydia Rutter;

Aimee Sawyer; Kate Sharp; Mary Beth Vaughn; Karen Yohe; and Christine Zimmer.

My gratitude to my family—my husband and publisher, Rene, and our three children and nine grandchildren, for allowing me to share the rich storytelling—and advice-giving—that I share with you. I cannot express how much my family means to me and how our shared experiences has given joy, and stories that will last for generations, to our lives! So, thank-you for your support and patience! And, finally, to Sven M. Dolling, my editor, for presenting this book in the best possible format, for all my readers.

Hugs from the Heart...

The Last Time

*From the moment you hold your baby in your arms,
you will never be the same.
You might long for the person you were before,
when you had freedom and time,
and nothing in particular to worry about.
You will know tiredness
like you never knew it before,
and days will run into days
that are exactly the same,
full of feedings and burping,
nappy changes and crying,
whining and fighting,
naps or a lack of naps,
it might seem like a never-ending cycle.*

*But don't forget...
There is a last time for everything.
There will come a time when you will feed your
baby for the very last time.
They will fall asleep on you after a very long day
and it will be the last time you ever
hold your sleeping child.
One day you will carry them on your hip,
then set them down,
and never pick them up that way again.*

Storytelling by Grand-Moms & Moms

*You will scrub their hair in the bath one night,
and from that day on they will want to bathe alone.
They will hold your hand to cross the road,
then never reach for it again.
They will creep into your room at midnight for cuddles,
and it will be the last night you ever wake to this.
One afternoon you will sing 'the wheels on the bus'
and do all the actions,
then never sing them that song again.
They will kiss you goodbye at the school gate,
the next day they will ask to walk to the gate alone.
You will read a final bedtime story and
wipe your last dirty face.
They will one day run to you with their arms raised,
for the very last time.*

*The thing is, you won't even know it's the last time
until there are no more times, and even then,
it will take you a while to realise.*

*So while you are living in these times,
remember there are only so many of them
and when they are gone,
you will yearn for just one more day of them.*

For one last time.

Author unknown

Hugs from the Heart...

*I know, intellectually,
that the fate of the nation
does not rest on a baby's poop,
but to keep sanity
and parents happy,
I must treat poop with respect.*

Poop Talk!

"You are all made of real poop." Anne Frank

Having pre-child conversations with adult children seemed like a million years ago! *How was your day? What strategies did you use to deal with your angry client? Do you have enough vacation days to cruise to the Bahamas?* Those were the days when parents were unencumbered by 'Baby Talk'! Nowadays, the first conversation with our adult children, straight through the door is, *"How many times did Baby poop?" "Was it gushy or solid?"* And without blinking an eye, the adult child's partner excitedly joins in the conversation!

When did we stray *so far off* the path to sanity! Poop talk sure doesn't make any sense to those people who don't have children. That stinky shade of brown and yellow poop, streaking up baby's back and smelling like a gaseous pile of cow dung, is of vital importance to parents, especially first-time parents! You check poop to make sure

Hugs from the Heart...

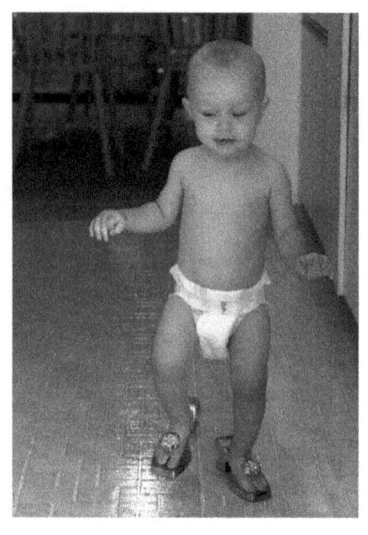

your child is going regularly *(what is regularly, if you are only four weeks old?)*, and you count the number of times each day that baby makes one. You follow up on consistency: *Was it too brown, not enough brown (...compared to what? ...your own poop?), too watery, too hard? Did Baby skip a day? Or did someone else (God forbid) change Baby's poop and not make a big deal about it?* Translated—forgot to tell you about the pooping process. *Did Baby grunt too hard or was it a sneaky poop? Were there any follow up smaller poops staining the diaper?* You, as parents, want all the detail. Leave *positively* nothing out!

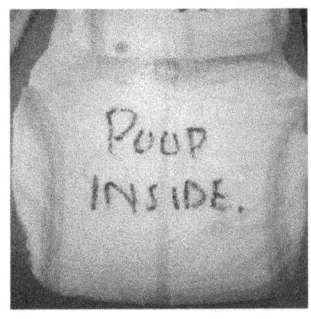

As a grandparent, I get grilled upon the arrival home of my adult children—home from their precious little time together. I try to ask them if they enjoyed their time out. I know that look—serious and yet pretending to be nonchalant, waiting for me to blurt out the evening's doings with Baby—first though, the pooping. What happened? Were there any gross poops that make for family folklore about a two pound poop combined with giant farting and Baby grunting? My adult children almost look disappointed if I tell them that all went well, the baby pooped, and we both went on with our lives. I always beat them to the punch with color, texture, depth, number of poops. Then the sigh! Ahhhh… All's well with the world as long as the parents get the scoop on the poop! And then, if the baby did poop, my daughter will ask, *"What did you do with the dia-*

per?" What did she *think* I would do with a dirty, stinky, poopy diaper? I guiltily tell her, *"I wrapped it up and placed it 'lovingly' in the trash, dear."* I am somewhat sarcastic. Not a good move to make light of poop! This is serious business that requires a serious answer. I laugh. Again, not a good thing. Maybe if I get the poop out of the pail and place it in the right pooping resting place, she'll forgive me for disrespecting poop!

I know, intellectually, that the fate of the nation does not rest on a baby's poop, but to keep sanity and parents happy, I must treat poop with respect.

I do know, for example, that poop reveals if the nutritional needs of the baby are being met. Poop indicates how a baby's liver is working. The milk stimulates the GI tract, which stimulates the liver and bile ducts and thus the yellow-brown color. Usually, formula-fed babies have a bowel movement a couple of times a day and breast-fed babies at least once every several days. But that can be different too. And the GI tracts being immature can account for *anything goes* in the poop business. Remember, that every child is different; some small babies are large-sized poopers and some large babies poop less often. But it all comes out in the end!

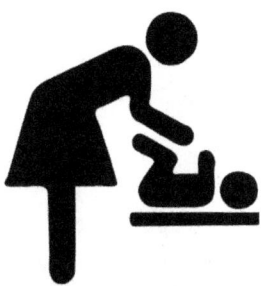

Poop Talk is important business for parents to discuss with important people in their lives. It can tell a keenly aware parent, whether a child is sick or well. It is more important to be aware of just how frequently your baby poops, so you can get some 'juicy' tales to tell baby when he/she is older—'Poop Tales.' *Place Poop in Perspective*. Soon you will be talking about *Pooping in the Potty*, but that's another story!

Hugs from the Heart...

*I find it
somewhat metaphorical
that Andrew chose
'Singing in the Rain'
as his performance piece.
While some would seek
shelter from the storm,
Andrew chose to
'dance' in the rain that day.*

Dancing in the Rain

"Children need to be reminded that their challenges do not define them." Anonymous

By Amy from Massachusetts

We are all faced with challenges in life, but how successfully we navigate through those challenges largely depends on how capable we view ourselves to be. Dyslexic children learn fairly early on, that their peers are able to conquer tasks that are seemingly insurmountable to them. Even the brightest students find themselves shirking opportunities to participate in class for fear of being wrong or worse, different. Unfortunately, many of these students find themselves focusing all their energy on their weaknesses. Unless these children are allowed to also celebrate their strengths, they will find it hard to develop confidence in their own abilities.

Our son Andrew is a very bright, inquisitive, little guy, but not long after beginning first grade, we noticed his light was dimming. His love of school first turned into like, but after a while, it turned into dread. It wasn't until Andrew began going to Landmark that we saw his light begin to return. Day by day, we felt our son was coming back to us.

One day after school, Andrew was especially eager to ask me something. As soon as he saw me he said "Mom, Landmark is having a talent show. Can I do it?" Of course, I said yes immediately. Naturally, I assumed he would choose to play the guitar, since he had been doing so since the age of four. However, when asked, he replied, "Nope, I want to dance." "Dance—did he really just say he wanted to dance?" Since dancing was something Andrew would have previously avoided out of fear of embarrassment, I asked again for clarification. Of course, he confirmed that I had heard him correctly, and began deciding what form of dance to perform. At that moment, I was both thrilled and scared to death. Here we were. Andrew was finally feeling at home again. He felt smart and liked and... happy. Although I feared what could happen if Andrew's performance was not, shall we say, appreciated, I feared more what would happen if we did not support his decision.

The day of the performance, my hands were sweating and my heart was in my stomach. "Please let this go well," I kept telling myself. Andrew proudly stepped out on the stage and began to dance. The more he danced, the more I relaxed, because I knew that Andrew was truly confident and happy. He finally felt safe enough to put himself out there in front of his peers, and fortunately, they did not let him down. The support Andrew received that day was absolutely amazing. In fact, I would call it life-changing and he would too.

No one is able to get through life without challenge. In fact, many times, the challenges we face allow us to discover our strengths. Children, however, need to be reminded that their challenges do not define them. When provided

Hugs from the Heart...

with the opportunity to also showcase their gifts, and feel the praise that comes from doing so, children will begin to experience themselves as capable. The byproduct of those experiences is confidence, which is an essential ingredient in the formula for academic and social success. Looking back now, I find it somewhat metaphorical that Andrew chose 'Singing in the Rain' as his performance piece. While some would seek shelter from the storm, Andrew chose to 'dance' in the rain that day.

Hugs from the Heart...

*Names are treasures,
if we take special care of them...
so that when our children
have grown old,
they will still smile
when someone calls
their name out loud!*

So, What's in a Name? Plenty!

"What's in a name? That which we call a rose by any other name would smell as sweet." William Shakespeare

I've bought houses a lot quicker than new parents can pick out a name for their unborn baby. Sure, it helps if you know the sex of the child. That eliminates 50% of the stress!

You don't want your child to have an acronym that spells out anything weird, so **F**redrick **C**harles **K**erby is out—***FCK***—too close for comfort! Or **E**lizabeth **A**nn **S**ally (after your grandmother) **Y**arger, or ***EASY*** for short! Particularly when she goes to high school where there is already enough peer pressure to have sex as it is! With initials that spell out **EASY**, you just know she'll be hunting you down!! And it doesn't look good either, when she graduates from business school and you have her initials carved out in gold on her new, expensive, leather briefcase! Think, parents, before you leap! Elizabeth is a lovely name. Perhaps you could compromise with Grandma Sally and your mom, Ann, and switch the initials. Then you can sleep at night. Who's going to make fun of **ESAY** on a briefcase? The worst that will happen is that everyone will think she can write an essay well!

And what about those baby name books and baby-naming websites. Sick of all of them too? Don't want to give your child the popular 'name of the year'? Now you can even check your own state to find out just how 'in demand' your name choice is this year. *Wikipedia* will tell all! Let's take Florida for the most popular male name. That would be 'Jayden,' and number two would be 'Jacob,' followed by Ethan, Michael, Mason, etc. In 2012, the most popular boy's name in all the states was 'Mason,' so if you named your son 'Mason,' and you wanted to discipline him in the mall for misbehavior, you'd say, "Mason Adam Divine, come here!" *Tricked you!* You forgot, those initials spell *MAD*, and that's your first mistake! Your second mistake would be to call your child only by his first name, 'Mason.' In this case, most of the other little boys in the mall would come running to you—a very popular name, indeed!

If you had a girl, and loved the name 'Emma,' you'd have the same problem in almost any mall in the entire United States from Massachusetts to Mississippi—kid you not! But it's a great name. Actually, my great-great-grandmother's name was Emma, and so was my husband's Grandmother! It does withstand the test of time! So, go bold, and popular, if you love the name.

How about, if you wanted to name your child

after a celebrity that you admired? Jason Lee, a pretty funny dude, named his child 'Pilot' after a song he heard by the band *Grandaddy*, called, *"He's Simple; He's Dumb; He's the Pilot."* And what about the name 'Apple,' the child of Gwyneth Paltrow and Chris Martin? At least they had a sweet reason (no pun intended)—"because it was sweet and wholesome," is the reason they gave. And the list of equally ridiculous names goes on and on and on and on! Look it up! Oh, you probably already did that! Please, please, please think, before naming your baby. The name may sound fine at the time, but long after you have departed this earth, *that* name will live on.

And then there is naming your child after a family member or someone in your *Ancestry.com* family tree. That would be best. Whenever you say, my child was named 'Stone,' for example, you can quickly lay a disclaimer on a person by delivering the deep-roots-in-the-family-tree spiel! That, honestly, can be one of the best legacy's you can leave your child. The gift of connection... the gift of belonging... to a lineage of people of whom you can then show pictures and discuss stories, passed down through time. That name is the connection to your past... to his/her past... and to the future.

Parents, you should always have the last say in naming your child. I know you agonize about it and make the best choice you can. You want your new family to be distinctive, so how about a nice compromise? For instance, choose the first name to match your new family's needs. So... you got pregnant at Deer Island, so you name your little girl 'Deer.' Then, for balance, with such a different name, take the opportunity to honor your family tree, either yours or your husband's or partner's, and give her a middle name which reflects the connection and respect for someone special in your family. So maybe, 'Deer Jane'— Jane, after Grandma Jane. I admit it is a bit weird, but with a name like Deer Jane Jones, at least the initials are respectable (DJJ)! And with any

luck, her classmates will call her, D.J.!

Names are treasures, if we take special care of them. Our children are branded for a lifetime by their names. Parents, it is a huge responsibility to craft the best name possible for your little one, so that when they have grown old, they will still smile when someone calls their name out loud!

Hugs from the Heart...

*Autism... takes everything
to a different level:
You see a cloud; they see art.
You see rain; they see tears.
You see a mountain;
they see a new world.*

Silence

"Autism is like building a home with lots of windows but not many doors." Paulette Buco

By Paulette from Iowa

Interesting, how silence can be deafening. It proves that we need the everyday noises to know we are alive: from the buzzing of the fly in the bedroom at night, to using an electronic megaphone, to the beeping of the microwave when it has completed its task, to a child's chanting to get our attention.

My granddaughter loves to tell me to "sit down"—like *I wouldn't love to*. It is so important to her that I am within eyesight. Her mom worked on potty training her. I tried, but it was truly hard and her doctor gave instructions as to what would work on an autistic child. God bless him, it worked. It worked so well, in fact, that she's trying to potty train *me* and her dolls—and there are very few accidents with her dedicated vigilance!

Needless to say, she is my bathroom monitor and inspector every time I need to use the restroom. There's no escaping. I've tried distracting her, tiptoeing around her, slipping into the downstairs bathroom to evade her 'inspection', all to no avail. This procedure includes outside restrooms as well.

I am under the impression I must become invisible. Once I waited until she was asleep to take a bath, quietly gathering my bath things. It was heaven for about three minutes. Then it was the attack of the rubber ducks, who, I might add, have creepy eyes. Like a Hitchcock movie, the curtain drew back and pajamas and all, I had a companion in the tub! *So much for a relaxing bubble bath.*

No yelling or screaming, except for the laughter! She thought she was being helpful—*not quite*. We dried off, got new pajamas on, and read a story before falling asleep, *that is*, both of us sound asleep!

I believe reading and talking about a story is important. You get to see a child's perspective. Autism sees the world so wondrously and differently. It takes everything to a different level. You see a cloud; they see art. You see rain; they see tears. You see a mountain; they see a new world.

It's sad when they become overwhelmed and their brain can't process. Sometimes, the meltdown is a day or two away. Meltdowns are hard: sometimes they need a hug, which grandma never runs out of; sometimes they need to self-soothe.

The unpredictability of life clashes with the need for similarity or sameness. It amazes me that she recalls every crayon. One missing is a *code blue*. She loves routine. Sometimes I fear OCD (Obsessive Compulsive Disorder), but I try to add variety and try to make it acceptable. I mix things up intentionally, the alphabet, the numbers, a song.

But, she catches it, proudly corrects me, and continues on. *Autism is like building a home withlots of windows but not many doors.*

Hugs from the Heart...

*The 'Time-Suck' hits
when you least expect it!
It's a sucker punch —
one that throws your
perfectly scheduled day planner
dead on its ear!*

Storytelling by Grand-Moms & Moms

Lost in a Television 'Time Suck'

"Theater is life. Cinema is art. Television is furniture."
Author Unknown

So I read this editorial in the *Boston Globe* about things that *'Time-Suck'* your life!

Let me back up a bit. To define *'Time-Suck'* is easy; to avoid it is a tricky mine field! Anything that takes over your day before you have the chance to notice your day is gone is a *'Time-Suck.'* It's silent and insidious, *and* addictive!

For example, not long ago, I flipped the television channel to *TV Land* and noticed a *Brady Bunch* all-day-and-all-night marathon. Normally—in fact, almost all the time—I would just wax nostalgic about the good old days of the *Brady*

Bunch and then keep flipping the channels for the next half hour (which is, in itself, a major *'Time-Suck'*). This time, much to my shock and bereavement, I noticed the reason for the marathon. Alice, the *Brady Bunch* housekeeper, and dearly beloved by the *Brady Bunch clan*, and all her beloved fans, had passed away at the tender age of 88 years old.

Where did the time go? My flashbacks to the early '70s seem indelibly etched in my brain. Can she have gone from 40-something to almost 90 in some television time warp, and I didn't even recognize it? That makes me—umm—never mind!!! But I digress from my original thought. Well, in between the tears and loss, for Ann Davis, for my own memories of the *Brady Bunch*, and raising my own children, for humanity's loss of such a sensitive and loveable housekeeper, well, you guessed it! I started watching Alice tributes, in one-half-hour segments from 6:00pm to 10:00pm. By the time I really noticed what I had done, I had been engulfed full force in a major *'Time-Suck'*! And then what? I felt happy that I had been with her, as a fitting and proper tribute to her memory, but angry at myself, that a half hour of remembrance was not enough.

The *'Time-Suck'* hits when you least expect it! It's a sucker punch—one that throws your perfectly scheduled day planner dead on its ear! The most common *'Time-Suck'* for me is finding the perfect television show to watch. So I take the remote, and to save time, I press the red button to see the guide. I scroll down the screen, sometimes a page at a time, instead of just one by one (I'm proud of myself for saving time!), yet I can't seem to find the perfect program that I won't waste my time watching.

"I hate people who are time wasters," I tell myself. I am efficient at my use of time, even in my television watching. So I continue—page after page after page after page.... Sometimes I stop and press the information button to read the summary of exactly what I will be watching on *NCIS* or some other program. I don't want to

waste my time if I don't think I'll like the content of the program, yet I am willing to watch reruns of *NCIS* just to see the cute, dysfunctional things Gibbs will do to Tony Denozo (my personal favorite)! That's a *'Time-Suck'* within a *'Time-Suck'*—double *'Time-Sucking'*!

My goodness, is there no end to my wasting time? Well, now that I've determined that maybe I will come back to channel 31, I continue to scroll pages well into the three hundred numbers, even though I clearly know that I cannot get any of these channels. I then decide to go to *Xfinity* and see what I may have missed last week on my favorite programs! Maybe I can catch a particularly fun episode of *NCIS* where Abby does something really cool!

So now, I must decide between regular cable *NCIS* or *Xfinity NCIS*. I choose *Xfinity* because I feel like I actually chose the episode tailored to my viewing need. I then begin to watch the program on *Xfinity*. I used to be able to fast forward through all the commercials to save time, knowing I am wasting it on some unconscious level. Now, there is a disclaimer that *"Fast Forward Button MAY be disabled."* That means I WILL have to watch all the commercials and that I will be in a conscious *'Time-Suck'* hell! But I justify it with, "At least I can mute the commercials". Now I have another *'Time-Suck'* within a *'Time-Suck'*! Double *'Time-Suck'*! Yuck!

So, in the end, I have *'Time-Sucked'* for three hours—although I thought I was being methodical—flipping through the channels with my remote, both traditional channels and *Xfinity*, and watching the one 60-minute episode of *NCIS* where I had no control over fast forwarding, although I DID have the power to actually rewind to the beginning; thus I could, theoretically, *'Time-Suck'* through an additional 60 minutes, should I choose to!

I wish I wouldn't have read that original article about *'Time-Sucking'* in the *Boston Globe*! I know I would have been a lot happier! I never used to think that much about how much time I actually wasted. And that's just on the television flipping and re-runs. Imagine how much more time I managed to *'suck'* up into the universe, never to recover! I should be ashamed of myself. I will be—as soon as I check out what's on TV tonight!

Hugs from the Heart...

*Here was a child that,
two years ago,
could not make a sound,
could not hold a pencil or crayon,
could not feed herself;
yet here she was,
on this stage
with her Mom, singing —
every other word, at least.*

The Butterfly

"What the caterpillar calls the end of the world, the master calls a butterfly." Richard David Bach

By Paulette from Iowa

Sometimes tears are not necessarily sad. They can capture the inner feelings and are droplets of emotion. Today, my granddaughter graduated from kindergarten. As a grandmother, I find myself regressing in time to when my baby daughter graduated from kindergarten. I watched and applauded, laughed, and cried. My mind drifted, like a time machine, to the past, present, and future—all at once.

I watched the K-kids perform with such gusto and heart, my eyes peeled on my granddaughter. She followed closely the steps and actions of her classmates but occasionally went her own unique way, a teacher reeling her in to the moment. She was definitely not having stage fright and danced up a storm when told to dance freestyle. She had rhythm! When they called her name for her diploma, she eagerly arrived onstage with a bounce in her step and a steadfast determination in her stature.

I saw my granddaughter *and* my daughter on that stage, together. My pride and the emotions flooded over me. I watched my daughter tear up with pride. Such an accomplishment. Here was a child that, two years ago, could not make a sound, could not hold a pencil or crayon, could not feed herself; yet here she was, on this stage with her Mom, singing—every other word, at least. She was dancing and socializing. My granddaughter worked hard to get here, but I have no doubt she'll go farther. I saw it that moment on the stage, the moment that captured her like a caterpillar emerging from her cocoon, taking flight. She, at that moment, turned into the most beautiful butterfly, taking flight, on that

stage, with her Mom by her side. Every day is one more challenge, one more victory, requiring of us, her family, time, patience, and understanding. But most importantly, love and family support has helped her fly like a butterfly, here, there, and everywhere.

Hugs from the Heart...

*The need to have
this baby is NOW...
you're constipated;
you pee your pants
any time you
sneeze or laugh;
the baby is kicking you —
but now it's not cute anymore!*

How do You Know when Your Baby is ready to be Born?

"I ate two waffles, a banana and cereal with blueberries. And that was between my two breakfasts!" Amy Poehler

All the preparations are complete. The baby's room is ready. The crib sheets are on, the black-and-white mobile is up, and the suitcase is all packed and directly by the front door—*check!* You have both clocked the mileage to the hospital *and* the time to get there during rush hour and in the middle of the night—from your front door to the entrance of the hospital door—*check!* The house is childproofed with all the 'thing-a-ma-jigs' securely placed into all the electrical outlets—*check!* You have a contingency plan

IF dad is not at home when the baby is ready to arrive—*check!* —in fact, you have more than one contingency plan—*double check!* You have the neighbor(s) feeding the dog, the cat, and the fish, when you leave for that trek to the hospital—*check!* Now what?

The WAIT! The Wait! The Wait! Your doctor has assured you that **"You will know,"** when it's time to have your baby; after all, he's delivered ten thousand babies. But he's male, so how does he really know? You're conscientious and have asked what seemed like a million questions: How can I tell the difference between false labor and the real thing? What about my water breaking? How much do I expect, a little trickle or a gusher? Will I embarrass myself if I'm out? What does it smell like? Water? Some of my friends have said it has a skanky odor, like lighter fluid. Is that true? How long do my contractions last at the beginning? When I'm timing my contractions, what is the magic amount of time between contractions—before I take off for the hospital? Should I wait at home, until contractions are—ten minutes? Five minutes? Two minutes apart? None of the above? If my baby doesn't come by the due date, should I be worried? After all, I have worked right up to the due date and now I'm just waiting.

If you, as a first-time mother are sick of all the myriad of unanswered questions and the doctor's reply of *"You'll know; don't worry,"* take heart! There is safety in numbers, after all. No one knows but baby, when 'he'll/she'll' decide to come. Actually, baby is already beginning the slow process of worrying you before birth, and this constant worry continues until 18 years of age and *well* beyond! Let's take this doctor's advice of *"You'll know"* apart and analyze it.

First, he's never had a baby, so right off the bat you know the advice seems not well grounded. He doesn't know the answers to these questions, so he can weasel out of them by giving this generic statement – *"You'll know!"* If you aren't satisfied with this statement, well, the first thing I would do, would be to buy ice cream, and while you're sitting on the couch anyway, at least you won't feel guilty feeding your face. Place the clock close to your comfy chair and watch the seconds tick by, as you eat your favorite ice cream and ask yourself, why for the life of God the doctor doesn't have better answers to simple, well-thought-out questions!

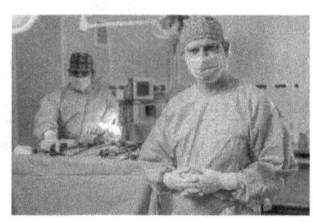

Second, if he's helped deliver so many babies, why can't he give you a more precise birth date for your first child? He is able to tell you that the eviction date from the womb for your baby won't be longer than... one week ...or more from the actual due date. That's great! But it doesn't help you with all the moment-to-moment worry and jitters you are experiencing *NOW! Everyone* you come in contact with, asks the same question: *"Haven't you had the baby YET?"* And *"When do you think he'll come?"* Well, if you knew the answer to either of those questions, you would probably have told them—dah!!

You have no restrictions on you other than you shouldn't fly, but you don't dare venture off far from home as it could be "any time now". Baby now has the upper hand, and he's not tipping it! Everyone is offering you tips for nudging baby from his secure resting spot! Your closest friends are now secretly betting on your due date. Someone's going to get a boatload of money as eviction day for baby is fast approaching, so there are only seven more days until 'D-day.' You can hardly wait.

The need to have this baby *NOW*, is fast overtaking the worry and nervousness you once had. Your acne is kicking up; you have washed your hair *every* day, 'just in case'; you're constipated; you pee your pants any time you sneeze or laugh; you haven't had a good night's sleep in months; the baby is kicking you—but now it's not cute anymore! It hurts. He's sitting squarely on your bladder, so you always keep the bathroom door within eye sight, wherever you go! And traveling anywhere now makes you queasy! You vow, never again to have another baby!

Fear not! When the actual blessed event occurs, and when you actually hold your precious baby in your arms for the first time, 'mommy amnesia' kicks in, and you **will** forget all the aches, pain, and worry you had! And bonus: **Your doc was right all along!** You *DID* know when to go to the hospital.

Listen to and trust your own body to let you know when baby will arrive. You've done everything right. But for now, kick back with a big bowl of your favorite ice cream and eat the whole thing—while you're waiting!

Hugs from the Heart...

*And like every milestone,
it has come,
and it has gone.
I am happy.
She is happy.
And I am happy
for her happiness.*

Storytelling by Grand-Moms & Moms

The First Day of School: Quivering lip?...or Pep in the Step?

"That it will never come again is what makes life so sweet."
Emily Dickinson

By Kate from Scotland, Mom to three small children

'The first day of school.' Some newbie school parents will read that statement with quivering lips; others with the enthusiasm of an over-caffeinated cheerleading captain. Some newbie parents will wonder where the time has slipped away; others will be excited to finally see that mythical empty laundry basket—or for new beginnings. As the days ticked down to my oldest's first day, I pondered which team would I be on? Team *'Sentimental Saps,'* or Team *'Tough Guys'*?

Being a newbie, I wasn't sure what to expect on the first day. How would I feel? How would she feel? How would I feel about how she felt? (Yeah, I tend to overthink sometimes...) As a stay-at-home Mom, I have thought of my daughter Lily as my right-hand girl these past five years. She witnessed first-hand my parenting highs and my parenting disasters—or learning moments to be kinder. We have kinda been learning this parenting gig together, as a team... What was this first day going to bring?

As dawn broke that first day morning, the buzz in the house was epic. With full tummies, pressed clothes and our (overdone-Pinterest-inspired) photo session done, I made the family walk me to wave our girl off onto her new journey. Watching the range of emotions from fellow newbies, I recognized the common denominator. *Whether it was a quivering lip or pep in the step, the first day of school is as big for parents as it is for kids.*

And like every milestone, it has come, and it has gone. I am happy. She is happy. And I am happy for her happiness. (There I go again...)

What have I been up to, with my new-found 'free time'? Well, I am off to—(hide the mess) turbo clean for the impromptu play date that is always lurking at the end of school, (chuck ingredients into the slow cooker) prep a healthy dinner, and slap on war paint, I mean, touch up my makeup before I do the school run. Don't get me started on school gate Mom code... ;)

Hugs from the Heart...

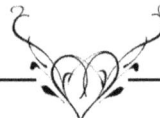

*We might have even
kissed a frog,
and then eaten an apple —
without a thought
to the number of germs
we were ingesting,
all because we didn't
give a damn about germs.*

There's More to Life than Worrying about Germs!!

"Having children is like living in a frat house — nobody sleeps, everything's broken, and there's a lot of throwing up!" Ray Romano

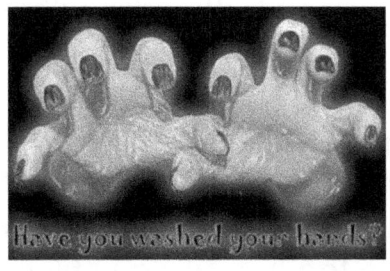

There, I said it out loud! There's more to life than worrying about germs. We live in a germ-phobic world! Maybe it's the overabundance of media scare tactics at every turn! Television tells Mom to wipe down the counters and all appliances with potent, 'germ-busting' products. Let's face it, I think we've created a sterile world. The only problem with our obsession about sterilizing everything is we have created an artificial environment, or bubble, for our kids to live in, that could be causing them even more problems in the future.

Who doesn't remember the ten-second rule? Remember, if it drops on the floor and you pick it up immediately—within ten seconds, 30 seconds, you name the number—that it was perfectly OK to put it into your mouth? Or, maybe your eyes would dart in every direction to make sure no one was looking before applying the ten-second rule, or if they were looking, you'd shout, "It's the ten-second rule," and everyone would nod their heads knowingly, and you'd get back to life as usual. You turned out fine! Pretty hardy, in fact. Maybe too hardy! You still have plenty of sick days that you haven't even taken at work.

Isn't it OK for your kids to lick a few germs once in a while—all in the name of good health? You know I'm right. You wish I weren't, but you were remembering back to that piece of candy you ate off the floor when you were a kid, or to the lollipop or ice cream cone you passed around so everyone could have their turn licking it at least once! Those were the days! Good old childhood days, when dirt was dirt.

Remember when we weren't so insulated from dirt. We could play all afternoon "until the lights came on" (remember those days??), and then come in and pretend we washed our hands for supper. We might have even kissed a frog, and then eaten an apple—without a thought to the number of germs we were ingesting, all because we didn't give a damn about germs. We thought they were a part of life, dirt and all! Life was too short to worry about germs. A good washing behind the ears and a hot bath once a week, on Saturday night when the heat was turned up and everyone in the house took a bath one after the other—sometimes two to a bath in dirty water so as not to waste hot water—well, that was considered best practice in cleanliness.

Now, fast-forward to parenting today, where baby resides in a virtual house, lovingly scrubbed down and disinfected from all known germs. And yes, we now have given formal names for germs that we try our best to eradicate: There are spiral shaped bacteria called spirillums; spherical bacteria known as cocci; and rod-shaped bacteria known as bacilli, all lurking in every crevice and orifice on earth, from soil to water to plants to radioactive waste!

But here's the $64,000 question. No matter how hard we try, could we or should we try to eradicate germs from the face of the earth? Let's face it, germs have been around for a gazillion centuries, long before man, in fact. Newsflash: Germs will be around long after man is gone! And a bonus question? Can't we all just get along? Instead of disinfecting and sterilizing everything our children come in contact with, suppose, Moms and Dads modified their stand on germs. We purposely inject viruses into our body to build anti-bodies to fight disease—so can't we find a way to co-exist with just the right amount of germs?

Quick: Check your purse, or baby bag, mom! How many pocket-size 'hand sanitizers' do you own? And how many did *your* mom carry around with her when you were young? We may be creating a world, where we have not been exposed to enough dirt and healthy bacteria to ward off colds or allergies. Check the number of children today that have allergies to just about everything, from environmental allergies to peanut allergies. I'm not saying that all allergies can be prevented with a healthy dose of germs, but I am saying to use common sense with your child and your household. Do wash hands, but use warm soapy water without anti-bacterial soap. Still sing the *Happy Birthday* song, so the child will follow good hygiene practice and wash hands long enough to be effective.

But do not obsess unnecessarily about germs. It is a dirty world out there, so sanitizing the Wal-Mart cart is still a good idea, but those places under your control, such as the home-front, well, you could be a little less abrasive with the anti-bacterial cleansers. Try vinegar to disinfect toilets, to scrub down countertops, to wash windows, and then make a nice salad dressing with the rest of it!

Prudence and level-headedness should prevail when it comes to fighting germs. Use simple, natural products without harsh chemicals. They are the best. I have pretty much given up all abrasive household cleaners. I use vinegar for just about everything. Anything harsher than vinegar should be stored outside your home, maybe in your shed? All bottles and cans leach chemicals which can get into your air conditioning ducts and circulate throughout the house. Those lovely scented candles and air fresheners that make your home smell artificially clean—pitch them and just open your windows, if you dare! The fresh air is really addicting! Keep it simple when it comes to cleaning and protecting your children from germs.

And remember a few germs can go a long way in offering protection. Build up those antibodies and your child will have more fun at play! And don't forget that, if that pacifier falls on the floor, and you pick it up and suck

the germs off before you give it back to baby, I'm watching you! And it's OK!

Hugs from the Heart...

*Let me tell you,
sprinkles will be found
into the next century!
They were everywhere
in the crime scene.*

Magic

"A house needs a Grandma in it." Louisa May Alcott

By Paulette from Iowa

Mommies are cupcakes with frosting; grandmas are cupcakes with frosting and sprinkles.

My grandchild has a challenge. I don't ever think of it as a disability, but it is a challenge. I am proud that she accepts the gauntlet each time. Frustrating sometimes for everyone, but we overcome. Once I found the key to opening her mind, it got a little easier. Her key is *numbers*.

On rainy days, it can be a challenge. I should have a bald spot on my head, I scratch so much to think of something both fun and helpful. Usually I'll ask: "What would you like to do today?"

The answer is a deafening silence, and a look like, *you're the grownup don't ask me*.

Well here was the situation the other day. I live in tornado alley where the thunder was really going strong, as it usually does in the Midwest. I think because of the lack of mountain ranges; the thunder seems to roll across the county like a train. Keeping her distracted and calm this particular day involved doing something magical.

Yup, baking!

I had her first separate the cupcake papers—lovely pastel colors of pinks, yellows, greens, whites, and blues. We laid them all out on the table and wherever there was an open space. Then I asked her how many were green? How many yellow? Then we commenced with, *if I take away one or two, how many do we have now?* This went on for a bit, and we laughed at the excitement of *just simply knowing*.

Next, the bowls came out, as well as the milk and eggs, and we mixed our batter. We cracked the eggs gently and looked at the yokes staring up at us from the flour. Our fingers traced a smile under the two yokes before we mixed it all together.

Of course, we had to do the little finger test to see how the batter tasted. It passed! With a spoon, we filled each cupcake holder to the top. The oven set, I went to get her camping chair.

Her job was to sit on the camping chair and wait for the magic. The cupcake pan slid onto the shelf in the oven, and I turned the oven light on. Taking personal responsibility for the magic, she watched through the glass oven panel as the cupcakes slowly baked.

As the cupcakes began to rise, her eyes opened wide in excitement, *"najik, najik,"* she shouted. Trying to pronounce magic gets her every time. Those **m's** are a challenge.

"Hide your teeth, mmmmmmm **magic**," I said to her.

And she tried: *"mmmmmmmm,* **najik***,"* she said for magic.

"OK, you tried," I replied. "Times up! They're

done now. We have to wait until they cool to frost." As time stood still, she fidgeted.

We made our frosting, got our spatulas ready, and began frosting our still-warm charges. As the frosting melted onto each cupcake, she was so proud of her magic! Let me tell you, *sprinkles will be found* into the next century! They were everywhere in the crime scene.

They were the most scrumptious cupcakes—mainly because of the *magic of love*.

Hugs from the Heart...

*It's in the pathway
of oncoming planes!
Can you not hear them?
Don't pick that house!*

Which House will They/We Pick?

"For the two of us, home isn't a place. It is a person. And we are finally home." Stephanie Perkins

If you're an *HGTV* fan like I am, *that* is the question we devoted fans of *House Hunters* ask ourselves routinely during the last two minutes of every half-hour segment.

We've followed the happy, and oftentimes *highly critical*, couple on their odyssey to find their perfect dream home! A home in which they can grow old together... raise their family together, make babies there to fill the house with

laughter and the patter of little feet. Their life-long plans unfold right before our eyes, as we learn their likes, their dislikes, their budgets, their inner struggles—well maybe not their inner struggles—but we do seem to make that deep connection with them. We even want what's best for them. As viewers, we are even willing to sacrifice our own taste in houses for the good of what the struggling couple wants.

And now we agonize with them. Can they possibly reduce their three favorite houses down to two? Can they eliminate one? Maybe one is over budget? *"You'll be house poor,"* we admonish them. *"Been there, done that,"* we chastise. Yet they persist in picturing themselves there, grilling on the large patio, with the outdoor stainless steel kitchen, and entertaining 50 of their closest friends with steaks and lobsters. You *know* they can't afford that house, let alone all the entertaining this house demands.

Or…*"It's next to a major highway; don't pick that house,"* we scream at the television or computer. Yet they stand in the backyard on tippy-toes, looking up at a row of tall arborvitae and a ten-foot-high fence while listening to sirens and honking vehicles speed down a major highway at 80 mph. We're hoping that telepathy, and our sane, objective voice will be heard by this couple.

Or…*"It's in the pathway of oncoming planes! Can you not hear them? Don't pick that house!"* But they seem to be distracted by the beautiful stainless steel appliances and the open floor plan they've always dreamed of, and *oh-h-h…* look at those beautiful granite countertops! *"But wait…!"* we shout. *Those damn granite countertops can always be placed into your more budget-friendly home later. For God's sake, be practical. You don't want to hear jumbo jets at 3:00 am, do you?"* Oh, no! They're smiling contentedly now. We *tell* them. We *plead*, ever the voice of sanity and reason.

Or… *"Hello! Why is no one listening to me? Your dream home is on a winding country road, winding its way into the middle of nowhere! And, you'll have a four-hour commute to work—one way,"* we tell them. And that's from experience, since we've made that same mistake before—ourselves.

Indeed, we have their backs throughout this entire house hunting process—*if* they would only have the common decency to listen to us, that is.

My *HGTV House Hunter's* moment happened this past summer as I searched in Florida, for the condo of my dreams, my forever condo (at least for six months each year)! I laughed out loud, when I realized that I was playing out a movie trailer from *House Hunters* over and over in my head.

Having seen three distinctively different condos, and looking for my dream condo where I could entertain both family and 50 of my closest friends, I knew then and there that I had crossed the line into reality television—in my own life! I was now role-playing an episode of *House Hunters*—but in real time, in my own life! And I couldn't get the ticker-tapes out of my head.

My dialogue went something like this:

"Well, dear, I think we should eliminate the most expensive one. It's way over our heads, budget-wise. I loved the condo on the second floor, across the street from the harbor. It's right next to where our daughter's childhood friend lived, in this lovely town.

But, there's only one major problem. They don't accept two dogs. Shall we write them a letter telling them we will be good stewards of this condo and lovingly restore it? Then we can slip in the part about having two dogs, instead of the one dog with the 35-pound-weight restriction? Oops! We have two dogs, but together they both equal the 35 pound weight limit. We can't possibly live without our dogs, both of them. Max is old, almost 100 years old in doggie years. Shall we ask for pet amnesty for Max? (We actually did write that letter!)

Hugs from the Heart...

After all, there are only a few units in this condo complex, and three of them are on the market. I really want to put a bid in on the second-floor condo. But it's only got a peek-a-boo view of the harbor? But it's such an awesome view from the second floor. We could offer a cash deal. Fingers crossed that they might allow us to bring our two dogs with us.

That leaves the condo in The Gardens. *It's reasonably priced, and all completely renovated with—BONUS—granite countertops (yay!), and all 'real' wood cabinetry! And it's on the first floor with loads of light and a lovely view of trees. And it's walkable to downtown and the Fisherman's Village. Did I mention, they don't have a problem taking two dogs? They also have a heated pool—which the last condo was missing!*

It's settled then. We both know which one we want. Are we in agreement? Let's tell Kate (our daughter). She'll be so excited.

Swear to God, that's how the dialogue went. Just like Cameron Diaz in the movie, *The Holiday*, where her job is to write movie trailers, and she can't get them out of her head.

Fingers crossed. ...and think good thoughts. Our real-life movie trailer plays out in a couple of days. *Stay tuned—"Which house did we pick?"*

Hugs from the Heart...

*I think Grandmas
are great big pillows,
especially during storms.*

And So the Wind Blows

"I am not afraid of storms, for I am learning how to sail my ship." Louisa May Alcott

By Paulette from Iowa

I think Grandmas are great big pillows, especially during storms. A storm can be frightening. I guess they can be frightening to grownups, too. When I was young, whenever there was a storm, the family huddled together and got through that nor'easter, or hurricane, or thunderstorm. Thunderstorms were the most frightening, as I think back on it. I remember my mother telling me the angels were bowling and every time they were up, God would take their picture with a flash! The imagery made me smile! Back then, there were only flash cameras. *But*, it made the storm seem less frightening.

Today, we had a doozy of a thunderstorm, as we do in the Midwest. It shook the house to its core. Those bowling balls must be heavy. One of the neighbors, frightened herself, came over with her child who was paralyzed with fear. My granddaughter picked up on it. So Grandma went into calm mode. I retrieved the secret stash of hidden jelly beans and M&M's, and I started to create. In no time we were gluing, singing, and laughing.

We sat a bit, and I had the two children create a story. Then I told them both a story until they fell asleep to the sound of the rain. The story was about the raindrop who couldn't fall. Once upon a time, high in the sky, there was a beautiful cloud. The cloud floated all over the world. It would change its shape over playgrounds so that children could see different wonderful things: rabbits, ducks, elephants, teacups, even teddy bears. It loved to hear the sounds of children and watch their imaginations at play.

One day the wind blew the cloud far over the ocean. This made the cloud sad. As she floated, the sun began to shine brightly; it began to heat the surface water. This made the cloud bigger. Then, droplets of water began to stick together—as clouds. One droplet of water asked the cloud why it was sad. The cloud told the droplet of water that, because of the water, the cloud could not move quickly and get back to the playgrounds and the children, and if it did, it would only make rain, and there would be no children to dream.

The wind started to blow harder and harder, and the cloud twirled and bounced across the sky. The little raindrop held on, while the bigger raindrops fell, splashing into the ocean. Almost all the raindrops fell.

Then the wind began to blow gently, and the sun began to shine. The cloud floated gently over a park. The cloud was so happy to see the children. They all looked up and pointed with smiles on their faces. The little raindrop proudly stood high in a rainbow in the sky, while the cloud smiled and gently passed by.

Hugs from the Heart...

We go to the docs
and the first thing
we tell people is
how our baby stacks up.
"He's in the 82%ile for weight
and 50%ile for height."
Against who?

My Baby is 14 Months, 15 Days, and 8 Hours Old!

"Love can change a person the way a parent can change a baby — awkwardly and often with a great deal of mess." Lemony Snicket

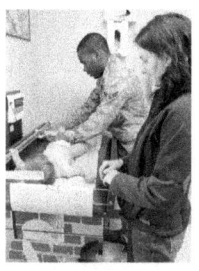

Why do all parents tell you the exact age of their babies, in months? ...or weeks? Instead of "My baby is 14 months old last Monday," how about, "My baby is a little over one year." Why are we so preoccupied with charting the number of weeks and months our child is, from the day he/she was born? You should know how old baby is! You participated in his/her birth!

What is the mystique of charting Baby's life to the day? By the time they get to be teenagers, you will be asking yourselves, "Where did the time go?" …or "He's getting so old?" You'll then chart the stages of life by the year in school. Did you ever hear the parent of a fourteen-year-old say, "My child is 168 months, 15 days old?" We don't even say the number of years any more. We say, "He's a teenager!" or "He's entering freshman year of high school." Your teenager still has ages and stages of growth and development as a teenager, *but now* it's more like you try your best to somehow make it through the teenage years—without losing your mind!

But for now, babyhood is magical, especially your first child! You have that pile of '*How baby grows*' books on the coffee table for easy reference, or you have some *app* on your phone to give you appropriate activities to sync to baby's stage of growth at 14 months.

There are charts of the 'average' times. You know what I mean! The average time it takes to…turn over from front to back and then to front again…average time to toilet train. If it's a boy add about six months more to the chart! …average time to read. It used to be six years, six months, but now with *Baby Einstein* and competition to be wait-listed at Harvard, it's more like six months, six weeks. We go to the docs and the first thing we tell people is how our baby stacks up. "He's in the 82%ile for weight and 50%ile for height." Against whom?

What are your babies being normed against? Who are they competing with, anyway, at 14 months of age? So, if your child is only in the 50th percentile in height should you be concerned since your baby is, obviously, 'average'? Why not place him on a rack and stretch him for a couple of hours a day? I'm just kidding, of course. But that's how silly all this norming is. If your child is in the 82nd percentile in weight does that mean you should be proud of him because he is fatter than 32% of the baby population? ... or should you place him on baby lock-down and ration out his food until he gets back to that 50th percentile?

I do understand that there are guidelines or benchmarks by which we keep a close eye on Baby. But we, as a nation, have gone too far. We live by the guidelines, forgetting that Baby is going to do and be just exactly what he/she is! No more, no less. And that should be fine with you, as parents.

Always challenge just where these benchmarks are coming from. If it's from doc, ask him when these guidelines were established? Are they current, relevant to your baby? We in this culture are proud to be parents of babies who are taller than the average, even though height should be irrelevant, except if lack of growth is a danger signal for baby. I am concerned at the amount of time parents spend in obsessing about height and weight and training time for pooping. I am sure, doctors are alerting parents to the average in the hopes, that parents will use these growth benchmarks as a means of observing wellness in baby. Sometimes benchmarks are just that, nothing less, nothing more.

Live your life with your baby in wonderment! Look at just how miraculous each day is. No two babies are exactly alike in their age/stage growth and development. It is possible to learn more through observing your baby and through your instincts as a parent than by any chart that the doctor gives us as a barometer of health and wellness. After all, nobody knows your baby the way you do. Use the benchmarks as suggestions, and use your own best practices to help baby develop into his/her own special self!

Hugs from the Heart...

My husband, daughter, and son were all sitting down to eat, and suddenly my daughter blurted out in a very matter-of-fact manner, "Daddy, your belly is big."

Kindness

"I really love being human. But some days I really wish I could be a fairy." Greta, age 4

By Karen from Florida

As a mother, one of the most important qualities I want to instill in my children is kindness. Kindness costs nothing, but the return on it is priceless. However, sometimes, I do fall short, as was evident in a conversation with my three-year-old daughter at dinner one night. What followed was as classic as an Abbott and Costello sketch.

My husband, daughter, and son were all sitting down to eat, and suddenly my daughter blurted out in a very matter-of-fact manner, "Daddy, your belly is big." My son, who was five at the time, found this hilarious.

I was indeed horrified, but used to her saying such things as she was three years old, and that she was the one in the family who has a broken filter. Nevertheless, I felt it was my duty to try to teach some empathy. So, while trying not to laugh, I said,

"Sophia, that is not very nice! What should you say to Daddy?"

To which she replied, "Daddy, I am sorry your belly is big."

I started to raise my voice at this point, because as all mothers know, when your children don't understand what you mean you should just scream it.

"Sophia, when you say that, you hurt Daddy's feelings!!! Please apologize!"

"Daddy, I am *very, very* sorry, but your belly is *REALLY* big."

Apparently, size does matter.

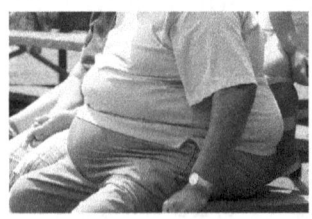

Hugs from the Heart...

*Remember all those
catchy articles
in Glamour magazine?
"10 Ways to Beat
Those Baby Pounds Back,"
or " 11 Ways to
Get in Shape in 30 Days
after Having a Baby?"
Only the Celebrities
seem to beat those odds!*

Reflections in the Mirror: I Am My Mom!

"Give every day the chance to become the most beautiful day of your life." Mark Twain

Change the perception of ageism in our popular culture, and you change the image and attitude of millions of women over 35! I'm not saying that 35 years old is *old,* mind you. I can't even remember when I was a mere babe of 35! What I do remember—*then*—was checking my face for crow's feet, almost every single time I passed by a mirror.

Women, you know what I mean! That's when it begins, creeping like spider veins around your eyes. You may even have bags forming from sleep deprivation, *and* they never go away if you have young children. They just turn a darker shade of gray!

Or, heaven forbid, the first signs of 'age spots' from your pregnancies, or the sun. You have slathered on the sunscreen with a low factor, like 3, instead of heeding your Mom's warning and trying the 100 protection that you brought to the beach for your own children, lest they get burned. You have more to lose then just getting sun-burned! Now, that lovely golden tan skin brought to you by suntan oils and tanning booths, is becoming tough, thick skin, and it may even feel like a cheap leather chair. It didn't occur to you before, when you tanned for prom, or spent every weekend in your bikini directly in the noon-day sun without that old lady floppy hat on. It didn't occur to you when you spent those spring breaks non-stop in that bikini—that you might someday come to regret those carefree college days.

Or, heaven forgive me, what about those pregnancy stretch marks. You remember, don't you? You thought you could outfox Mother Nature as your stomach grew to the size of the biggest beach ball every used in a beach volleyball tournament! They lied to you when they gave you tips for keeping the stretch marks at bay in *Cosmopolitan* magazine. You couldn't cream them away with the most expensive stuff ever made on earth—made just for such a purpose. Or with any fad creams, coconut oil, aloe, or whatever the tip was at the time. Remember all those catchy articles in Glamour? *10 Ways to Beat Those Baby Pounds Back,* **or** *11 Ways to Get in Shape in 30 Days after Having a Baby?*

Only the celebrities seem to beat the odds. And that's just who turns up on the cover of those magazines. Amazing! If I only had a personal trainer come to my well-equipped gym for six days a week. Or if I only had the 40' by 60' indoor pool with pool volleyball and 90 degree water. Or if I only had my own personal chef to prepare me those fabulous dishes meant to take off the baby fat, all in under 150 calories a day. Maybe you could lose like those airbrushed celebrities with personal plastic surgeons who redesign their butts and eviscerate their stretch marks, or perk up those sagging boobs, tortured to death by breast-feeding on demand by three kids.

Yeah! That's what it takes, yet we keep looking for the *magic bullet*. We keep looking for the one magical 'thing' that will come along to will us pre-35 again! But there's nothing that will take back the years! It's all smoke and mirrors, and it takes months of hard work and hours of precious time that we must divide in more ways than we have hours in the day!

And *terrible* bonus for young women over 35 years old: Since we live in the age of technology and instant communication with family and friends, we now must contend with *Facetime*! I want to throw up when I see exactly what I look like on that nasty magnifying glass of an invention, and I'm lots older than any 35-year-old! If you are like me, you try to text instead. *Facetime* magnifies every single pimple and gray hair on your head. *Facetime* instantly sets the women's movement back 50 years! *Facetime* is no one's friend.

When my grandkids see me on *Facetime*, they see a kind old lady who loves them dearly, AND, an invention that ages me beyond my wildest dreams—taunting me that my skin is not anything like my young grandchildren, or my adult children, but more like some alien from another planet. I try my best, but don't like it. Period.

Even taking selfies, nowadays, women over 35 try to instruct their moms (me), to stick my head forward in some ostrich-style pose, then in some awkward, convoluted move, retract my neck up and backwards, while holding my head and neck still, staging a smile while my head is just at the right angle, tongue inside willing the double chin up, up, up! But if I am really lucky, I might land smack dab in the middle of the selfie in the back row. Each year I slide further and further to the back of the family group selfie, especially if I'm with my daughters. They may be in their 30's and 40's, but they are already feeling the veins straining and cracks creeping up their faces.

Hugs from the Heart...

And, bonus, they look into the mirror and actually see themselves growing into their Mom's faces. I remember the first time I cut my hair short. I was around 35 years old, and thought I looked hot! *Then*, praise Jesus, I looked into the mirror that the hair stylist gave me to admire his handiwork and my short, sophisticated, with-it style! *Holy S***!* I was exactly, positively, without a doubt, the spitting image of my Mom, and the signs—double chin, sagging mouth, the deep wrinkle crease between my eyes, well, it took my breath away—*and my will to live!*

I look back on that day, and believe me, a woman remembers exactly where and when that happens, and I remember in Technicolor all the details, and laugh. My mom was a bit overweight at 60+ years old—maybe horizontally challenged more than I realized at the time, but she was beautiful to me. I accepted her flaws and all. Her round barrel-like shape, her droopy mouth, always looking like her dog had just died, the fine short straight hair—with very little gray, I might add. Even the gestures, the arms on hips (not that she could find her hips or anything), the look that could kill from across the room when she was pissed at me. I had it all—when I turned 35!

The more I tried to ignore it, the stronger the urge to keep staring at her. What was I missing? What else would happen to me! But the clothes she wore, well, that, in itself, took my breath away. She was always a very conservative dresser—until she hit a certain age, somewhere around 60 years old, I believe. Out came the big oversized shirts from the local department store—in wild leopard prints. She had polka dotted shirts, bright orange Caribbean-style shirts, and those stripes! She bought them in black-and-white—my personal favorite for her! She also had wild travel shirts—and she never traveled anywhere but through books! She had her Paris Eiffel Tower shirt, her safari saber-tooth tiger shirt, and *so* many more shirts, lined up in her closet.

When I finally asked her how on earth she could have the guts to wear such wild colors, she said: "Women become invisible at a certain age. It's a youth-centered culture, my dear. So I want to make sure I never become invisible to anyone." Words of wisdom I never forgot, since I, too, now wear wild neon-colored shirts and wild yoga pants. It's the fad now, but thank God! Otherwise, after a certain age, that's just what happens, a woman becomes invisible. Mom didn't have anyone else who wore those types of wild shirts, but she sure wasn't invisible.

She also wore over-sized Bermuda shorts, you know the Cargo shorts where you can slip 50 packets of *Sweet'n Low* from *Denny's* or extra chicken wings in large napkins directly off the Chinese buffet easily into your pockets! To say I was mortified, was putting it mildly! It drove me mad! But who's going to challenge an old lady on a mission to stock her house full of restaurant food. No one, that's who!

Here's the greater question in this whole *get-*

ting-older-and-feeling-bad-about-being-who-we-are thing, brought on by this *youth-centered culture*: Why do we let pop culture dictate who we are, how we should act and dress at a certain age? And for goodness sake, why do women over 35 years old feel the pressure to spend their last pennies on packaged garbage that promises to eviscerate age?

In some cultures, age is a badge of honor. We shouldn't want to turn back our age to feel good about ourselves. Yet we spend trillions of dollars buying s***, just because we are over a certain benchmark age, artificially contrived by a youth-crazed culture! We can't reconcile ourselves to a few well-deserved wrinkles. All the movie stars, even the men, plasticize themselves to death, scrape down the wrinkles and all we say is, "They look so good!" Why, if you had that much done to you, and filters to soften whatever wrinkles were left, you would look like ten again too!

Women over 35 number in the tens of millions, so why can't we stop—just stop! Let's bring the cosmetic world to its knees! I mean, a little lipstick can't hurt and maybe some mascara, and even some eye-liner, but cut the crap. Cut the make-believe wrinkle eraser, and buy some coconut or olive oil and massage that into your body. No chemicals, no 'natural ingredients,' which, translated, means anything the cosmetic industry wants to add to it, over 200 different chemicals. Let's just stay natural, close to the earth, dance in the moonlight, and do yoga on the beach without sunscreen. Let's take our gender back and, at any age, relearn what it means to be beautiful!

Hugs from the Heart...

*Quinn sets her own agenda.
She is a high-functioning
autistic child.
She will find her niche,
but we just have to accept
what that looks like.*

Quinn

"Kids have to be exposed to different things in order to develop." Dr. Temple Grandin

By Paulette from Iowa

Suggesting a journal is always a wonderful idea. As the Grandmom, I had started one when my granddaughter Quinn was born. Like everything in the hectic life of a Grandmom living with her active daughter's family, it fell by the wayside. It's hard writing to yourself. I guess it's easier for me to share feelings.

This morning when I opened my Facebook, I got a pleasant surprise. My daughter actually wrote about what she believes her daughter is going through. It was a pretty accurate description.

She wrote: "Imagine going to a really loud rave with tons of lights that are annoying. Imagine people moving past you really fast and asking you questions, but not waiting for your response before asking another, or ignoring your response altogether or saying 'what'? And making you repeat yourself three or four times. That's what things probably look like from Quinn's perspective at times. Most of you would crack under these conditions, but she handles it like 'boss' every single day. I look up to her; I mean she is an easy person to be around, despite all that is probably going on in her pretty little head."

It, I believe, is a great interpretation of autism. I believe, both Gabby and her husband have accepted the diagnosis, but have a hard time accepting what it entails. I see them wanting desperately for her to be a 'normal' child. It will take time, and she will function at her own pace. However, not the way we expect.

Quinn sets her own agenda. She is a high-functioning autistic child. She will find her niche, but we just have to accept what that looks like. We can't make her something she isn't, just guide her in the right direction. Give her wings, and eventually, she'll takeoff.

Quinn is excellent in math, reading, art, music, and has a phenomenal memory, too. She's getting there little by little, working on her social skills. She doesn't shy away from kids, only when they want to strike up a conversation, probably because they don't understand her. Once she has the enunciation of her words down, she'll be fine. It takes patience.

I'm so proud of her accomplishments. I'm teaching her to use a laptop. Why? Because it gives her dexterity with her fingers as she spells out words. She can type her name, Mom, Dad, Seth (that's her speech therapist), and she asks to learn new words. She's still in progress, baby steps, as they say.

It took long hours and 24/7 constant repetition, of hand over hand, listening to the sounds, but once she has the sound or word, she owns it.

Quinn is special in more ways than one. She can make you laugh, cry, and when I am with her, her energy and determination make me happy to be alive.

Hugs from the Heart...

*Sometimes less is more!
That's an old adage,
but truly appropriate!
Children today
have too much 'stuff'!*

Rethinking Toys

"If little else, the brain is an educational toy."
Tom Robbins

It's Christmas Eve and you're busily wrapping that mountain of presents after your toddler is asleep. All is prepared for Santa's arrival. You made delicious chocolate chip cookies and decorated them with your toddler—*check!* You've read *"Twas the Night before Christmas'* with your child on your lap—*check!* You've filled Baby's embroidered stocking with loads of goodies to eat, and small stocking stuffers (which you spent more on than on some presents)—*check!* You've bought the boatload of presents—some educational, some board games, some more, more, more—lost track! In fact, by the time you've wrapped the last present, you've lost track of what's in all the other wrapped packages. It's impressive though! Why, the mountain of presents makes you the best parent this Christmas—*for sure!* But are you really sure about that?

Sometimes *less is more!* That's an old adage, but truly appropriate! Children today have too much 'stuff'! Their bedrooms are filled with toys from the time they are infants. The more-is-better syndrome is insidious. We just want to be good parents, but buying more may not be the way to get baby's attention.

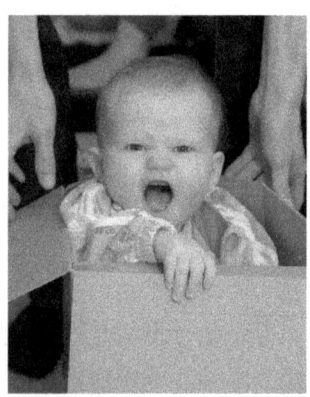

In fact, I bet if you give your baby two pots and a couple of ladles and spoons, your baby will entertain himself for hours on end. It will be loud, but it will be creative. He will place the pans on his head, on the dog's head, on your head. He will try to step into the frying pan. That's where a couple of packing boxes come in handy. Watch while your child uses his imagination and places these boxes side by side, or one on top of the other, or gets in and out of the box for hours on end. He will cart his pots and pans into the cardboard box and then out of the cardboard box, over, and over, and over, and over! And he'll smile and giggle over his dominance of the boxes. He might even want to add a towel over the box to crawl into—a cave or a secret hide-out! Don't forget, if he can't see you, he believes you can't see him either. Remember peek-a-boo? Your child believes this concept of being seen and not, depending upon if he can see you!

So maybe, next time you wrap Christmas presents, choose the boxes carefully, and leave out the stuff inside. When your child sees the box itself as a present, he has truly chosen imagination, and that is the greatest gift you can give—a 'thinking' child!

That goes for birthday presents too. I have a friend who has simple birthday parties for her child. The toddler gets to invite three friends, and instead of the children giving the birthday girl presents, the toddler discusses with mom just what each child would like. At the party, the child gives each girl one of her toys, the gift of giving and the joy of sharing what she loves. And it works! So think about what really makes children happiest. It's the simple joys, the verbalizing how happy her birthday makes her feel, reminiscing "on the day you were born" to your child.

It's the planning of a simple party together. For example, I have another friend who had a book birthday party, in which each mom brought a special book that the child already owned, wrapped it up, and read it to the other children at the party.

Each Mom read the child's book, with her child on her lap, and they swapped books, so that when they left the party, each child had a different—gently used, but greatly treasured—book. Everyone had a blast, and the focus was on the joy of sharing and the reading of a beloved book, which they read and then swapped.

It's not the 'things' our children accumulate that bring joy, but rather the experiences they create with their family and friends through joyful discussion and expression that make for an unforgettable birthday or holiday! Try it!

Hugs from the Heart...

*I hope
we can continue
to do our weekly fun day,
long into the future!*

Favorite Pastimes with the Great-Grandkids

"If nothing is going well, call your [great]grandmother." Italian Proverb

By Lydia of Florida

From the time my three great-grandchildren (two girls and one boy) were three years old, I would babysit regularly for them while their parents were working. We always had tea parties, everyone, including the boy. It was the only show in town. They are now 5, 8, and 9 years old, and we are still having tea parties which they really look forward to.

Once a week, after I pick up my great-grandkids at school, they can choose an after-school fun activity, something to look forward to at the end of the school day. They each take turns picking a playground and a place to eat. Their favorite place, and mine too, is *Chick-fil-A. Bonus:* There is also an indoor play area to let off some energy after a hard day at school. I hope we can continue to do our weekly fun day, long into the future!

Storytelling by Grand-Moms & Moms

Hugs from the Heart...

*Oh, hexagonal pencil
made of graphite
and encased in a
thin coating of yellow wood,
topped with a
lovely pinkish eraser,
where have you gone?*

The Demise of the Pencil

"Memory believes before knowing remembers."
William Faulkner

Did you ever stop to think of what's become of the *pencil*? I always remember needing them for school. Remember, when you needed to keep three pencils on your desk, sharpened at all times?

...Or when, at the beginning of the class, or before school had begun, you waited in a long line to sharpen your pencils for the day?

...And the pencil sharpener, which was screwed tightly to the wall, would grind the yellow wooden pencils to the sharpest point possible—as you twirled your heart out, round and round. You would take it out of the pencil sharpener periodically to carefully examine the point. Was it as sharp as it possibly could be? Could one more twist of the handle produce an even sharper point?

Who has a pencil sharpener now? Even the electric, whirring pencil sharpeners seem like old technology today. Seems like the only thing we need a pencil for, and a #2 pencil at that, is for those high-stakes tests in school, or to evaluate your college professor at the end of a semester! But even now, most major tests are being transitioned to computer, not a #2 pencil. Doesn't that seem like a million years ago?

It all started somewhere in the mid-fifteenth

century. Yes, you heard me right. The first pencil was actually made in the mid-fifteenth century—with lead! That, in and of itself, was bad for kids. Then we began to use graphite, which was lighter and thinner.

And remember, as a kid you could actually buy your very own plastic pencil sharpeners in a variety of colors to place in your 'pencil box holder'? Oh, hexagonal pencil made of graphite and encased in a thin coating of yellow wood, topped with a lovely pinkish eraser, where have you gone?

It says in *wiki* (my personal *'go-to'* for a quick reference), that the graphite and wood are "permanently bonded—to the core". That is exactly how I felt about my pencil, bonded to the core of my being, indelibly imprinted on my soul. Well, maybe I've gone too far! But I do have fond memories of where my pencil and I have gone and how far we have both come!

Hugs from the Heart...

The pencil is all but gone as the writer's implement of choice. I broke away—no pencil pun intended—and upgraded my pencil to word processing and texting. I think of an idea, and I immediately take out my iPhone and jot down those ideas on my phone's notepad. I wouldn't be without it anymore. I write directly onto *Facebook*, *Twitter*, and, in *Pinterest*, I upload my pictures to take the place of actually writing words. My implement of choice has changed with the times, lest I become a dinosaur! And I won't have that!

Hugs from the Heart...

*I looked like something
from another world,
but she thought
I was beautiful.
Beauty is truly
in the eyes of the beholder.*

Storytelling by Grand-Moms & Moms

The Makeup Queen

*"Patience is not simply the ability to wait;
it's how we behave while we're waiting."* Joyce Meyer

By Jan of Florida

Having been a Mom to two boys, I was used to being outside having fun. They both loved to fish, camp, or do anything connected to water. I was in for a big surprise when my granddaughter was born. We were her babysitters for two to three days each week and were fortunate to see her many milestones. For her first couple of years, she loved being outside feeding ducks, taking walks, or just looking at birds. Then everything changed and she became afraid of all animals. Outside was no longer fun for her. Even walks were a little stressful as she cringed whenever she heard a dog bark or saw the ducks coming her way.

Around the age of four, she discovered makeup. She watched *YouTube* videos on how to apply makeup, as well as watching everything her

Mom did. It wasn't long before I became her favorite *target*. Her Dad or her Grandpa would do in a pinch, but they didn't like sitting to allow her to practice her new craft. She never asked her Mom to sit for makeup when she could get her Grandma to sit for her.

As she began to learn how to apply makeup, I found myself with gobs and gobs of makeup all over my face. If she couldn't find her blush, eye makeup or even lipstick worked in a pinch. Each time she applied makeup, she learned to use more control with the brushes. She became a collector of all kinds of makeup (from the *Dollar Tree* store) and tried all of them on me.

By the time she was five, she could put makeup on with more finesse than me. I could never put lipstick or eye shadow on with such precision. One day she decided that I would become Harley Quinn. Having no idea who Harley Quinn was, I was game for her to try. Little did I know that my face would be covered with layers of white makeup for a base. Then the colors and layers were added. Red lipstick made wonderful blush. She was so proud of her work. Needless to say, her grandpa kept his laughter to a minimum and videoed the whole thing so we would all have an everlasting memory of that day.

I looked like something from another world, but she thought I was beautiful. Beauty is truly in the eyes of the beholder.

Hugs from the Heart...

*Don't beat yourself up.
Remember, your infant
will only be this adorable
and tiny once!*

Moms: Can't Fit into those Size-2 Jeans?

"I remember right after the twins were born, having that weird jiggly belly and kind of loving that too — because I earned that jiggly belly." Jennifer Lopez

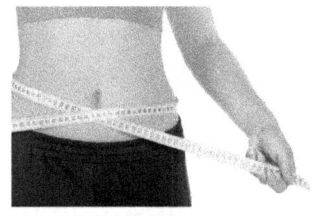

What's the first question new moms want to know—besides "Do I breast feed or bottle feed?" Some of you feel guilty even thinking the question. You may feel that all your attention should be focused on baby. Well, I'm going to ask that question. "How long will it take me to lose that 'baby' fat?" And if you're honest, you're also worrying about just how much of the 50-plus pounds are your own jelly belly weight? Even by my calculations, no baby alive was ever born weighing 50 pounds! That's a frightening thought, because you know, deep down, that 50 minus a 9-pound baby still leaves 41 pounds to lose!

But wait! If you pick up any of those fancy baby or parenting magazines, they will tell you—"10 Easy Ways to Shed That Baby Weight." Sounds like 'shedding' is the operative word. If you could 'shed' those pounds like a snake sheds its skins, you wouldn't need to worry! But it seems the older you are, and the fact that your hormones are raging, and the baby is nursing, and you just can't get to the gym at 6 am—since you're breast feeding at that time, and bonus, you're also getting ready to feed again. It seems, that baby is an eating machine. So how easy can it be to shed that baby weight?

And for goodness sake, **do not read** Cosmo or Marie Clare, or Glamour just yet. Doesn't it seem like the celebs, all the Hollywood starlets, don't miss a beat in shedding that weight? They float effortlessly on the cover of the most glamorous magazines—two months after Baby is born—shedding all their baby weight and more. If they can shed that, then so can you, right? Well, answer these questions: Where is your personal nanny for Baby? What about that personal cook who is preparing three luscious meals a day—all under 550 calories? What about that home gym, where you work out three hours a day with a personal trainer who comes to you? And the massages scheduled every day to ease the stress of Baby's needs? And the personal shopper, who brings outfits to your home so that you can bond with your baby, yet still look chic? If this idea of shedding the pounds appeals to you—*forget about it!* That's going to break the bank, and probably, you will not be any happier (I'm just kidding here)!

Instead, take a deep breath, and take all the full-length mirrors down, or at least turn them around so that you can legitimately not feel guilty about the baby weight gain. It takes about a year to shed the weight. Some women lose slower than others. Don't beat yourself up. Remember, your infant will only be this adorable and tiny once. So make sure you have a rocker in your bedroom or in Baby's room, and spend as much time as possible bonding, singing to Baby, and telling him how much you love him. Also, baby massage will relax both you and your baby. Especially when done after a warm bath—yours or his—and remember, that touch is the cornerstone of bonding! This is your time to understand what that little bundle is all about. Their cute traits and quirky little moves should be the thrill of your days! Nights too, if your child has days and nights mixed up—but that's another story.

The weight will come off, but be kind and loving to yourself. Society pressures us to bounce back too quickly, to stress about looks before we (or Baby) are ready. Your body will tell you how much you can do. The first month, be careful to pay attention to the joy of motherhood and do not listen or read anything which tells you otherwise.

When your strength returns, you will know, and you can resume activities and dieting. But until then, reach for those pregnancy pants—you know, the stretchy ones with the elastic bands which are forgiving and comfortable. You'll be back in the game before you can blink—but Baby's days with Mom are limited, so enjoy them!

Hugs from the Heart...

*My heart would break
without being part
of this family,
and without my
special title, 'Grandma.'*

The Art of Controlling Drama

"I take a very practical view of raising children. I put a sign in each of their rooms: Checkout time is 18 years." Erma Bombeck

By Paulette from Iowa

Being a live-in Grandma, has its share of additional challenges. I not only am Grandma, I'm chauffeur, cook, housekeeper, fashion coordinator, teacher, playmate, problem solver, therapist, sounding board, and, at times, the '911' go-to person of the household. Sometimes it seems, I'm also the dead horse to kick. Grandma is hated, loved and everything in-between. I thank God every day for the privilege. My heart would break without being part of this family, and without my special title, 'Grandma.'

Some say, "How can you stand the drama at *your age?*" Age? When you're active, it seems age is not a concern. Now when I say *active*, I don't mean I have to spend every waking moment running a marathon. It is the quality time that makes memories that count. Time spent with my grandchild *is* something I regard as a precious gift. That time is what breathes life into me. Time—something we can't buy or barter for, or guarantee. Every moment with someone you love is a treasure. The good, the bad, and, *yes*, even the ugly times are the footprints left behind. But the drama, ah!

Drama is an integral part of the workings of family. Knowing how to deal with the drama is an art in itself! I have choices: I can explode, be patient, or be a problem solver. I take after my dear departed Gram. My Grandma was a problem solver to the nth degree. My Dad was too. My family was one big, extended, happy family, navigating the dramas of an extended Italian family living together—day in and day out. *Drama was everyday life.*

When my aunt became deathly ill, it was Grandmother who kept everyone calm; she sat with her in the hospital, day after day, and listened to her patiently. She crocheted during the quiet times, and told stories so my aunt could hear her comforting voice. Then they moved my aunt to a critical care facility—she had tuberculosis, and back then, you were doomed and isolated. My grandmother would walk six miles to the hospital, literally! She'd pack her lunch, bring her crafts, and be right by my aunt's side. Silently she would soothe my aunt. When everyone gave up on my aunt, she didn't. Grandmother made her famous soup and fed my aunt every day. My aunt recovered, and she'll be 90 next month! Also thanks to Grandmother, my aunt became an awesome knitter, crocheter, and sewing mistress, thanks to Grandmother. Every Christmas Grandmother would make our dolls clothes, and each of us mittens, sweaters, hats or scarves. I believe Grandmother was the reason my aunt lived. Her faith and love was strong, and giving up was not an option to Grandmother. She was my strongest example of what a grandmother should be. Every time there is a 'situation' (code word for drama), I ask myself: "What would Grandmother do?"

Well, today's 'situation' was the bathroom. One has not lived until the toilet has been strangled with a roll of toilet paper. It made the most horrific choking sounds, as if it were in the throes of death. I think it's a fascination to watch the water swirl and digest the potty's content. I am convinced we have won the award for most water used in our state. There should be a plaque coming any day for the most toilet paper stuffed down the toilet by one grandchild. Luckily my granddaughter is potty-trained—amazing, it took only three days, and no real accidents since. But the amount of toilet paper consumed reinforces my resolve to be as patient as Grandmother was.

Today, after the fortieth flush and hand washing, I wondered if it was my Granddaughter's OCD (she is autistic on the spectrum), or was she just having fun? I had a brilliant idea. We had bought a potty chair, with a flushing sound; I moved it to the middle of the living room and placed a dolly on it. Ok, that solved the potty part. Now we also have a fancy ice chest with a faucet spigot which was given to my granddaughter as a gift. It now sits in the living room, alongside the potty. The ice chest releases water from melted ice. Voila! Pretend hand washing for the dolly and my granddaughter right in the middle of the living room. We are still working on the soap part, actually using soap along with the water. It's a work in progress, and adds another new dimension to the everyday drama.

But Grandmother would have been patient, and so will I!

Hugs from the Heart...

*The mother
of all intrusions
is entering into my
meditative space.
I am witnessing
this intrusion as if
I were invisible.*

The Intruder...

"If you want to conquer the anxiety of life, live in the moment, live in the breath." Amit Ray

I arrive at my favorite '*go-to*' spot, to spend time meditating. This is *my* special place to center myself. I watch contentedly, as the waves smash the granite rock formations at the ocean's edge, frothy tips swirling and slamming onto

shore. Dark clouds coat the sky, striations of various cloud formations in horizontal layers. It is truly the perfect setting painted onto the landscape before me. Navy blue waters speak of an impending storm as the frothy mist seeps into my nostrils through the small opening in my car windows.

I am parked perfectly, within the appointed white lines, back end first, front facing the vista. I am prepared to enjoy the moment. My pre-set radio station is playing light classical music, and I have my green tea steeping within my Dunk's styrofoam cup. I am ready. I recline my seat. I open my windows further, for some chilled New England air, and meld the raging of the ocean's rantings with soft orchestral music. I taste the salt air and feel the textures of life through nature's music and Vivaldi's *Four Seasons*. I begin to delve into a deep meditative state.

...*UNTIL*, a very large truck parks horizontally against the curbing across the parking lot, obstructing my view. I endure, believing that he will not be there for long. Tolerance and a determination to stand my ground keep me in place, though not in my happy meditative mental place. The truck belches black fumes. Atop the open truck is one lonely, blue port-a-potty, with white trim, and the name of the company affixed to the potty *and* the truck.

I wait, practicing tolerance. I know it will pay off. Not another soul is in the parking area. A permit is required to keep nonresidents out. Not this time! After *maybe* ten minutes of belching fumes, the truck engine is silenced and a small, muscular man with silky pajama-like shorts hops from the truck, whistling. It looks like... *no... no... it can't be!*

Yes it is!

The mother of all intrusion is entering into my meditative space. I am witnessing this intrusion as if I were invisible to him. The driver is purpose-driven, mocking my meditation, though he does not know it. I am sure he is following orders, but *not here, not now!* I need this time, this inspiration, to center me for my day.

I watch, like a fly on a wall, waiting for the next step, which I know will happen—the dismounting of the throne upon the ground. In slow motion, I see all the steps involved. First, my intruder jumps onto the truck, removes the potty bindings, and effortlessly pushes the bulky blue structure to the edge of the truck. The potty must be surprisingly light, since the man is so small. I can't imagine why these port-a-potties don't tip over easily, maybe even when I'm inside, as I so often use them at outdoor concert events.

My mind wanders back to concerts, to the times I've waited to pee for what seemed like an eternity—waiting for the line to snake its way toward the blue relief bucket in the middle of the field. In those lines, concertgoers became life-long friends, even exchanging phone numbers as they waited for the potty, patiently. I always kept my eye out for the best potty to use, the one I *guessed* might be the cleanest? How could I even know that? Deep down I knew, none really were. They never had toilet paper left, or if they did, it was a lone roll that could have been God-knows-where—probably rolling around the floor! *But* desperate was desperate!

Then finally came the anticipated green light, the unoccupied sign. I could now step up into that black abyss and pee! It was finally my turn! But what if that surprisingly light port-a-potty overturned? The onerous smell said it all! I never looked down into the dank hole!

After today, I will never again mistake large and bulky for sturdy and weighed! I will tread lightly, and I vow to always pick a steady potty. Some of the ones I have used in the past, rocked and swayed, depending upon where I placed my feet.

I am brought back to the here and now by the restarting and cajoling of the large monster truck. I am in a daze, thinking now more about that port-a-potty than meditating in this beautiful spot. There is no one in sight but the port-a-potty man and me. He hops deftly from the truck and makes his way through the black exhaust fumes—without coughing or wheezing!

The port-a-potty man goes through his ritual, seriously, silently, whistling stopped. I do not exist! He does not pause to look my way, to gesture me in some way—any way—that he is sorry for the intrusion into my place of meditation. He does not pause to even acknowledge this place as a sanctuary, a place to tread lightly.

Rather, he goes right to work to Vivaldi and

the raging sea, ironically, in harmony with both. What he is about to do, does not fit this place of meditation and beauty. It doesn't even seem to matter to him.

He just works rhythmically and systematically; first dismounting the potty onto the tail lift, then placing it squarely on the blacktop—blocking part of my ocean view. Well, I reason in my *Nothing will disturb me, not even a port-a-potty* meditation. I reposition myself, and try to maintain my Zen-like state. But I am not feeling Zen-like; I am fuming, along with the exhaust from the very large and rusty truck. At least the bulky blue potty is off centered, to the left, with a perfectly wonderful vista straight in front of me, over the hood of my car. *I can co-exist with a port-a-potty*, I tell myself. I resume my meditation.

For God's sake! What is the man doing now? Unbelievable! He is prepping the potty, by placing blue crystal sanitizer within its bowl. I could guess it is a disinfectant, even from a distance.

Done! No harm, no foul—no pun intended. But now, the man is filling a large orange bucket with some liquid from a large semi-transparent barrel. I don't even want to guess what *that* is! Into the potty with the blue crystals. The only thing left to do is stir, but, I don't see a stick, thank goodness. Done now, finally.

I resume my meditation again, myopic vision—eyes straight ahead. Blinders on, to my left, I use the meditation tips I have learned to block out unwanted thoughts, to help me eviscerate the bulky blue potty from my world. No luck.

I begin, instead, to focus on the features of the port-a-potty. The curved arched top to help me feel less claustrophobic as I climb on board, sucked into the dingy world of goo and guck, just to pee! Yes, it does have the occupied sign. White trim outlines the entire bulk, adding design, much like trimming a house for occupancy.

Like a magnet, my eyes are automatically drawn to the potty, no matter what I do to obscure its view. Obviously, pretending it is not there isn't working.

The man, it seems, has completed his delivery. I thought... *UNTIL* he grabs the potty and lifts it completely off the ground. I actually smile. His jarring and lifting the potty is probably mixing the blue crystals and cruddy disinfectant together, part of his master plan, probably.

Where is the man taking the bulky blue potty now? *NO*, I scream silently, knowing the answer even before he drops it exactly into my sight line, completely blocking my view. *NO, NO, NO...* There is a small, slight, indentation in the paved parking lot, exactly in front of my car. He plunks that potty down in that exact spot. The intruder returns to his belching truck and drives off, his black fumes trailing behind him.

Only my potty and me—left! It is a sorry sight.

Now, I need to pee! I squirm and suddenly realize, I have no choice. The quickest place to go is... *OH, NO!* The potty stares at me. I think I see the green unoccupied sign winking at me, beckoning me to pee in its sanitized, unused potty. I do.

Hugs from the Heart...

*Just being around our grandsons
brings us great joy,
but taking trips as a family,
and bringing Pop-Pop
and Grammy along
to capture lifetime memories,
now that's as special as it gets!*

Storytelling by Grand-Moms & Moms

Let's Go on a Trip: Bring Pop-Pop and Grammy!

"Grandchildren are the dots that connect the lines from generation to generation." Lois Wyse

By Tricia from Florida

Traveling can be exciting and fun, especially when traveling with adult children and grandchildren. Seeing the world or other parts of the USA with a two-year-old and a four-year-old adds to the fun!

Our first travel adventure with two of our three grandsons was aboard the Disney cruise ship *Disney Dream* in October 2016 . We left Port Canaveral, Florida, for a five-day cruise to the Bahamas. Little did we know, that a hurricane was bearing down on us, directly in the path of our intended course! *Hurricane Matthew* was threatening to move into the Bahamas. We were told that there would need to be a change in plans. Our new destination was now—Mexico, which was fine with us. We arrived at the Disney terminal and the fun began as soon as the children spotted the first statue of Mickey Mouse!

The wide smiles on those little faces said it all! It was something I will forever remember. Upon boarding the ship, we went straight to the top deck to take in the best view, and also to find where lunch was being served. The array of food from which to choose went from dazzling to overwhelming, the length of two football fields! But, in spite of the luscious food selection, their first choice was *always* chicken nuggets and Mac-and-Cheese! We soon found our cabins, and it was time for the two-year-old to take a nap. His was the bottom bunk, a new experience for him!

The first night was fast-paced, with entertainment, more food, and a chance for our almost four-year-old to sleep in the top bunk for the first time. He was elated! Morning came early for our son and daughter-in-law, so we offered to take the kids to breakfast so they could sleep a little later. They suggested that we could also take the boys to a show right after breakfast which featured their favorite character, *Jake the Pirate!* We happily agreed.

This breakfast turned out to be hilarious. My husband suggested that we go to the 'nice' restaurant, the one with the tablecloths, fancy! But I was thinking that an informal buffet on the top of the ship would be more suited for two little boys with an appetite for finger foods, especially donuts!

I went along with Pop-Pop's idea. So, there we were, seated at a quiet table in a not-very-crowded fine dining restaurant with two adorable little boys, who definitely preferred chocolate donuts to eggs Benedict! Our waiter quickly took our order of Mickey's waffles, fruit, and scrambled eggs and bacon—just for the kids—*the children who preferred donuts.*

It seemed like an eternity before the food arrived, so little boys did what little boys usually do best to entertain themselves. They started to get a little rambunctious which quickly turned rowdy. They saw our waitress from the night before. Those little rascals don't miss a thing! She walked by our table with a dish piled high with donuts of every kind. And then they went ballistic with happiness. She was out of chocolate but promised she would be right back with their request for chocolate donuts. She kept her promise, and they soon had polished off two chocolate donuts in a flash—faster than *Jake the Pirate* could say *"Arrrrr."*

Now they were finished eating, *but* our food was just arriving. As two angelic children became bored, the fun was just beginning. Our quiet table soon became louder and louder. And, *BONUS!* They discovered that fruit can be more fun when one throws it at his brother. After few minutes of trying to stop the fruit war, especially after all the sugar was, by now, careening through their veins, I laughed and let them know we were leaving as soon as possible. *Fine dining might not be for two small boys with donut cravings after all.*

The next stop was the Pirate Party. We finally found its location and joined the small audience for even more fun. By the time *Jake the Pirate* arrived, the boys could hardly contain themselves. They were literally jumping with joy, so excited and happy. I nostalgically remembered back many years ago when our own kids were that little and how much joy we found in watching them, and on the adventures we had, as a family.

The music started, and the kids were encouraged to step up to the dance floor to join in the marching, singing, and dancing. The music was lively, and the boys had enough donuts to keep their energy going for a long time. Grandparents were encouraged to join in on the fun, so Grammy and Pop-Pop did just that! By this time, all ages were up and dancing, not paying the least attention to how we acted. What better way to have fun than with two little boys dancing their hearts out on the dance floor. I have to admit it—*it was so much fun!*

The rest of the week seemed to fly by, with all the memories we were making with our own children and grandchildren, altogether on *Disney Dream*. We soon received word, that our five-day cruise was going to be extended until *Hurricane Matthew* had cleared the East Coast of Florida. By the smiles on their faces, it seemed to be fine with everybody. I saw it as an opportunity to have more fun, make more memories, and spend more time with our two adorable grandchildren who live six hours away.

Our next travel experience happened rather quickly after the Disney cruise, about 8 months later with death of a family member in New Jersey. Our daughter decided to bring her almost two-year-old son to New Jersey with her. I was already there, but my husband traveled with them. We met up with our family and many other relatives who were meeting this precious little guy for the first time.

He was just an angel, who was happy most of the time. We stayed at an old inn nearby. He stayed in the portable crib in a room I shared with my daughter and baby. It was a joy waking up in the morning to that little smiling face. It really helped me cope with my grief. It was so comforting to see my family members interact with and enjoy him. And it reminded me of the cycle of life. At the funeral home they had a special room downstairs and the children in our family took it over. They ranged in age from two to 17 years old. Although this was a short visit, it was more enjoyable, because we had this little passenger along with us.

Recently, we spent two weeks with our two older grandsons on a trip to Ireland. They were really so well-behaved on the plane during the round trip, first six and then eight hours on a plane crossing the Atlantic. Our daughter-in-law brought lots of toys and activities to keep them busy. They slept some of the time in their car seats. In Ireland, we visited many different places, stopping frequently to climb or visit various sites. The boys were entertained easily, especially with some of the more simple things. Once again, no need for fancy, when simple, age-appropriate things pleased them the most.

For example, one day we visited a firehouse in Ireland. They were beside themselves as the firefighter showed them all around. He patiently talked about what firefighters do and was just amazing with the boys. He actually started the engine of the fire truck and gave them a slow ride around the parking lot, the boys sitting atop the fire truck in the cab. To their delight, he turned on the siren. Pure magic! Life couldn't get any better for these two boys and Grammy and Pop-Pop! They just loved it and couldn't stop talking about their visit to the fire station in Ireland.

Just being around our grandsons brings us great joy, but taking trips as a family, and bringing Pop-Pop and Grammy along to capture lifetime memories, now that's as special as it gets! My husband and I are blessed to have these three little people in our lives. We hope for a long retirement so we can have more fun, visit more great places, and sometimes just sit around and listen to them talk and laugh, recounting their forever memories with Pop-Pop and Grammy!

Storytelling by Grand-Moms & Moms

Hugs from the Heart...

*Children learn
through role modeling.
This baby learned
that nobody was going to
pay attention to him.*

Your Baby Deserves You... ALL of You!

"Forever is composed of nows." Emily Dickinson

Just today, I was in a coffee shop and noticed a well-behaved eighteen-month-old baby in a stroller; well, maybe not well-behaved in the usually sense of the word. But rather in a trance-like state, staring at an iPad for about an hour. Was he with an adult you ask? Well, technically, I guess you could say he was. An adult was physically present, but texting away on her iPhone. I think they were having lunch, 'together.' Well, maybe not exactly together in the communication, sensory stimulation sense of the word. More like, spinning spheres, each in their own orbit, never touching or colliding. I timed the 'lunch' from beginning to end. It was exactly 48 minutes, and during that entire time, neither made eye contact. I was fascinated. How could that type of a relationship foster communication—never mind, how cold and desensitized to one another they seemed to be—both mother and child.

So what does a little baby (and yes, 18 months is still a little baby in my eyes) need for a successful interaction and to foster successful communication? Focus and attention, I believe. I cannot imagine a worse lesson for this young child to learn. Isolation and the cold shoulder from mom! There were so many lessons the mom could have taught her child. First, the joy of being together. If there were only the mom and baby, and NO technology of any type for distraction, they would have 'found' each other—even if it were by default. Eye contact, an important part of communication and role modeling would have been fostered. Mom would be using her skills of listening and tuned into the needs of her baby, and she would have perhaps even given him words as labels for what he was eating. She also could have talked about how to eat food with a fork or spoon, or what manners were appropriate within the boundaries of a busy restaurant at noon time. The baby would have been engaged with learning... about his mom... about how to be a part of a larger crowd in a restaurant... about the joys of dining, and the mindfulness of being in the moment.

Children learn through role modeling. This baby learned that nobody was going to pay attention to him. He also learned that being entertained by the games on the iPad was acceptable behavior, even the norm, at the dinner table. He learned that mom was too busy with her games too. He learned that the stimuli from the world around him was to be tuned out. He learned that isolation and loneliness were the preferred ways of communication. He learned that non-verbal communication was not necessary a vital part of the overall communication exchange. He learned to fend for himself; his mom never looked up.

From where I sat, I saw a child whose social skills were already in jeopardy, and for whom school and all its social interactions would be a problem. I saw a mom who really didn't 'get it,' how important her time with Baby was, and her responsibility to be 'in the moment' sharing this important time with her son. I saw a little baby who would become a young man doing the same thing with his child, and thinking that was acceptable communication.

Ironically, I overheard this woman speaking on the phone. Her last words were, "I'll be home in about 15 minutes. Bobby and I are just finishing our lunch." Clearly, she will be the one, someday—way into the future, when little Bobby is in high school, who won't 'get' what went wrong with this lonely, isolated young man, unable to make connections with others.

Turn **OFF** your cell phone and any other electronic devices when having lunch—with anyone! It's insidious, this technology trap, and you won't realize the damage it does, until it's too late. Your baby deserves **you—all of you**... focused... attending to the conversation.... **You** as the teacher—**You** as the parent—**You** as the nurturer—**You** as the wise one, who knows what it will take to raise a socially well-adjusted child in this age of rapid and pervasive technology. As *Nike* says, "Just do it!" Your child deserves ALL of you!

Hugs from the Heart...

*He really thought
he had won,
but I was proud of him;
he was brave.
He knew what he
really had to do;
running away wasn't an option.*

Storytelling by Grand-Moms & Moms

Runaway

"You can't run away from trouble. There ain't no place that far." Uncle Remus

By Paulette from Iowa

I was a mother before I was a grandmother. Every so often I pick up a family album. Remember those books, before the cloud or iPhones? That was when cameras were used to take pictures to recall your memory when you get old.

Well, I happened to have saved one, and I nostalgically and thoughtfully reflected through the photos, trips we had taken, or birthdays of family members and friends, anniversaries, etc. Then I came upon my son's picture. I remember taking it with the Polaroid camera. I remember my words to him. He had been angry because he couldn't have an ice cream before lunch. He announced if that were the case, he would run away. I remember saying to him: "OK, but first let me take your picture so I can remember what you look like."

He then began to pack his little suitcase, the one he used when he visited Grandma. All the necessities, *Star Wars* figures, stuffed animals, and most importantly, a peanut butter and jelly sandwich, which he made himself with a full jar of peanut butter and half a jar of jelly. All this, stuffed in his bag. With a quivering lip, he announced his goodbye and left. I watched from the kitchen window, as he strode his determined walk to the gate, and opened it, which gave me a bit of worry.

I could see him fidget, but I knew he would go no further. I noticed he was about to come back. As he made his way back, I could see him mumbling to himself. There was a rap at the door, and with a stern voice he announced, "OK, I'll give you one more chance." Keeping my composure without laughing was a miracle.

I said, "Well, thank you, but you still have to

each lunch before ice cream."

"Okay, deal."

He really thought he had won, but I was proud of him; he was brave. He knew what he really had to do; running away wasn't an option. I clutched the photograph, and I smiled.

Hugs from the Heart...

*I'm circling the moon.
I don't know how.*

Circling the Moon

"We turn not older with years, but newer every day."
Emily Dickinson

I'm ready to fall asleep.
I'm ready to be released, ready to have some unseen presence sprinkle angel dust upon my body.
I'm ready to surrender into a peaceful slumber.

I lie here, millions of random thoughts darting, like the fire flies I used to try to catch, with my mason jar, three holes punched into the top and grass popping up helter-skelter, anchored by stones plunked down in the bottom of the jar. Fireflies flit and dart the way my mind does, waiting for the angel dust, not settling my mind.

I tug at the blankets, covering my fully clothed body, socks and all, and I drift off—

I'm circling the moon. I don't know how. I drift upon a cloud and flit about, blinking out messages in Morse code like the fire flies do, mimicking them from the moon and stretching my body in downward dog to view fire flies below. I am beguiled by them, under their hypnotic spell.

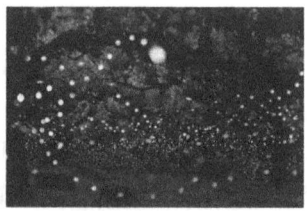

Both fire flies and I, stinging the black night with light, one dot matrix of hope, not insignificant.
Angel dust falls gently from the universe beyond, covering me in a sparkly cloak, aglow in silver, as millions of random fireflies blink from below, winking up at me. I float far above them, effortlessly around the moon.

Hugs from the Heart...

*It didn't matter,
where we went,
or what we did;
being with Grandma
was what was important...
I was the most important person
in her world that day.*

Storytelling by Grand-Moms & Moms

Grandmother of an Oldest Grandchild... Reflections, Past and Present

"Each day of our lives we make deposits in the memory banks of our children." Charles R. Swindoll

By Chris of Florida

In the 1950s and 1960s, I must admit, my life was pretty good. I was the eldest of six children, and the oldest grandchild of my paternal grandparents. They lived just a few miles away, and every Sunday we visited at their home. That was nice, but what I loved the most was when I had the special opportunity to do things with my grandmother—just the two of us!

Grandma would invite me to spend the night sometimes. The house had four bedrooms, and I got to sleep in the one across from the big bathroom with the claw-foot tub. When I spent the night, we usually had an adventure planned for the next day.

Hugs from the Heart...

My grandmother was a lady. She *always* wore a dress, and when we went out, she usually wore a hat and white gloves. I had my own little white gloves, and usually wore them and a dress when I went with her.

My grandparents did not own a car, so for our adventures we usually took a taxi. Sometimes we went downtown to the big department stores, and usually had lunch in the restaurant at the store. Other times, we went to a retreat center where she often volunteered.

It didn't matter, where we went, or what we did; being with Grandma was what was important. She talked with me about all sorts of things, and made me feel like I was the most important person in her world that day.

Now, around 50-60 years later, *I am* the grandmother! I have four wonderful grandchildren. Two live nearby, and two live in another part of the country. I have the privilege of driving my two oldest grandchildren to school once or twice a week. When I drop the younger one at the elementary school, I still have about 45 minutes before the oldest is due at the middle school.

I treasure this time with her. We have conversations about all sorts of things, but most of the time the discussions are about family, friends and faith. Sometimes we run errands, or grab a bite of breakfast. She is open and interested to many things. She's also fun and loving. Seeing life through her perspective keeps me young and interested in things that I may have stopped caring about decades ago.

This summer I have the gift of spending a week with all four of my grandchildren together, and most of the time their parents will be working. I'm calling it *grandma-camp!* The cousins love to be together, and it only happens a few times a year. I'm thrilled that I get to share this part of their lives more fully. I know that we will make memories that will last a lifetime, just as mine have of the time spent with my grandmother. Perhaps *grandma-camp* will become an annual event for the next 8-10 years as they grow to be young adults. I hope that I am that blessed!

Hugs from the Heart...

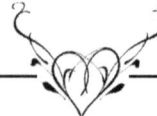

*Follow these Nine
Parent Coaching Tips,
and you will have
a well-prepared child,
who is more confident
of his or her
math abilities!*

Nine Parent Coaching Tips for Battling Math Anxiety

"Encourage and support your kids, because children are apt to live up to what you believe of them." Lady Bird Johnson

Remember this formula: Confidence + Solid Preparation = SUCCESS

Parents, with high-stakes testing here to stay, math is more challenging than it's ever been before. Follow these *Nine Parent Coaching Tips*, and you will have a well-prepared child, who is more confident of his or her math abilities.

1. Coach your child to develop a positive attitude!

One of the most important ways that your child

can do better, is simply by having a positive attitude. Don't let your child sell herself short by saying things like, "I can't do math; I am no good at math." If she believe she can do it, she WILL be able to do math!

2. Coach your child to ask a lot of questions!

There is nothing embarrassing about asking questions. Your child will *not* look like a 'nerd' to her classmates. In fact, her classmates probably want to ask the same questions, but they are afraid to ask! It could be, that the teacher is not explaining the math concept fully. Maybe the teacher can explain the concept in a different way. ASK!

3. Make sure your child doesn't fall behind!

Your child is building on a base of math skills and concepts. If she misses something early on, it gets harder to catch up later. Also, to take the next level of math courses, your child needs to master the linear concepts to be successful.

Try tutor services—professional ones, or try a high school student in advanced classes, recommended by the local high school guidance department. Do not wait until your child is failing. Consider tutoring as an investment, and sign her up as an additional booster for math. And keep her in the tutor program. If she already understands the concept, but feels a bit shaky, the tutors can reinforce and enrich her. Tutors can keep up by talking to your child's teacher, and sometimes they will be able to get a copy of the math textbook. Falling behind can lead to feelings of "why bother?"

4. Practice, Practice, Practice!

That's how we learn anything—*through repetitive practice*. Usually it is not until your child applies the concepts to real problems, that they 'get it.' Practice out in public. Calculate money everywhere.

Find a sequence or pattern of cars driving on

the highway, etc. There are life opportunities to show the relevance of math in your child's life. Coach her to find relevance in the 'real world.'

5. Build your child's confidence!

When she does her homework, start with easier problems, or problems you know she can do. Review simple ideas first, or material she covered a year ago. That will give her the confidence to approach the more difficult problems. Baby steps...

6. Coach your child to show her work!

It is tempting for you or your child to skip steps, but that does not reinforce the concept being developed. Remember the importance of repetition? It is better she gets into the habit of showing all of her work. That way, if there is a mistake, it is easier to see the mistake quickly and correct it. You can also detect a pattern of mistakes and help her immediately. Plus, your child may get partial credit for a tough problem that is *almost* correct.

7. Do NOT ignore wrong answers!

While accuracy is always important, a wrong

answer can tell you, as your child's coach, to look further to see if your child really understands the material.

8. Coach your child to write neatly!!

It is important that your child organizes problems, and writes numbers and variables clearly, so that she does not confuse either herself—or the teacher. Sloppy numbers equal wrong answers!

9. Don't be afraid to go low-tech! Use old-fashioned flash cards!

Don't be afraid to use the tactile approach. Symbols, equations, and concepts can get overwhelming. Use flash cards to organize information or test concepts. She can sort facts into piles, and watch the pile of "don't knows" get dwindled down. You can place unknown facts on the refrigerator, so your child sees them whenever she opens the refrigerator door.

Hugs from the Heart...

*We went into
the examining room.
All seemed under control,
until it wasn't!*

The Appointment

"I might hit developmental and societal milestones in a different order than my peers...small victories on my own time." Haley Moss

By Paulette from Iowa

A doctor's appointment can be traumatic for a child. I believe this is the norm. My granddaughter is pretty laid back about doctor appointments. She takes them in stride. She has them so frequently, that most likely she's conditioned to just accept them as part of her life. She has speech therapy twice a week and is nonchalant about that, too.

Well, when I told her that Grandmom had a doctor's appointment, she was so excited and couldn't wait to come with me. I worry about her thinking some times. Who but my granddaughter would even want to go to a doctor's appointment!

It happened that my appointment was on Monday, the same day as her horseback riding therapy. It was a bit out of the way, but close to where she needed to be when my appointment was over. So it was a family affair. My daughter, my granddaughter, and me! ...off to my doctor's appointment. Honestly, I was grateful, in a way, because it's always good to have two sets of ears at a doctor's office—my adult daughter I mean.

My daughter came with me and together we located the specialist's office. Quinn was wonderful on the way, excellent in the waiting room, until I was called.

We went to the examining room. All seemed under control, until it wasn't! When I had to leave the room for an X-ray, chaos rained down. My granddaughter seemed possessed. I could hear the screaming clearly, from down the hall. Now, I really did try to make this a positive experience for all of us. I thought I would be out in a flash. Not quite the way it worked.

By the time I got back to the room for the results, the ranting was in full force. She wanted me to sing *Jingle Bells*. This marvelous Harvard grad sang graciously off key, but it didn't help. It had to be a chorus line to please this child. After the show, somehow, we were having a conversation, of which I understood every fourth or fifth word.

Next appointment, I go alone. Horseback riding was a breeze. Grandmom was definitely traumatized.

Hugs from the Heart...

*What does
a red parrot
have in common
with stress?
Here's the test...*

Storytelling by Grand-Moms & Moms

Parrot Talk: Stressors that Keep You from Seeing

"If your Baby is 'beautiful and perfect, never cries or fusses, sleeps on schedule, and burps on demand, an Angel all the time,' you're the Grandma." Teresa Bloomingdale

Parents, what I want you to do now is **STOP**... stressing... and relax! The *Today Show* recently conducted a survey of 7,164 U.S. mothers which indicated that once parents reach "...a certain critical mass of kids, life seems to get a bit better." Three seems to be the point at which most Moms indicate the highest level of stress, 8.5 out of a 10-point scale. More than three kids, and the stress seems to diminish according to *today.com*.

But the common denominator is that 75% of all mothers say that they are stressed from within, not by outside pressure. Imagine that percentage of Moms stressing about the stress they feel within. It's crazy what pressure American Moms feel—and, I'm sure, Moms in other parts of the world feel that stress too! It's that need for perfection. Flash to all Moms everywhere! Perfection is unattainable, so use the same ten-second rule you do when your child drops something on the floor, and you dust it off and call out to the world, "It's the ten-second rule"!

Go easy on yourself! Parenting is a journey that simply MUST be enjoyed. The time is so limited and fleeting! Stress is real and may at some point, if left unchecked, cause you to miss out on the fun and enjoyment of those 'blips' in child-rearing. You know, the stories that later become legendary at family gatherings, and which are nostalgically embellished as the years go by!

OK, now for the question I know you are asking yourself: **What does a red parrot have in common with stress?** Here's the test. Apply the ten-second rule to the parrot. But this time, stop the madness, and **REALLY look** at the red parrot for ten seconds straight without worrying about what is happening around you. Hard to do? You will be rewarded with the illusion of the red parrot. Well, go study the parrot and come back before reading any further!

...Did you see it? Embedded within the red parrot is a dancer with outstretched leg (hint: the parrot's tail feathers). This dancer was body-painted and embedded within the parrot to fool you. Did it?

Now, examine what you did to actually focus on the dancer! You really had to let go of your perception of a parrot and look at the bird 'from a different perspective'! Now, consider stress and that grueling statistic of 75% self-imposed stress that Moms take on needlessly. You need to ask yourself this question: **Is the stress real? ...or is it self-imposed?** If it's real, 'deal with it,' and solve the problem causing the stress, either with a step-by-step plan, or by isolating the stressor and examining the impact of the stress on you as a Mom. Usually, when you examine your stressors, your anxiety lessens. It *will* turn out that 25% of your stress is real, and that 75%—as *today.com* concludes from their survey—is self-imposed.

Now, imagine Moms all over the U.S., who are empowered by examining their stressors. That will lead to a calmer, more rational Mom, who can really participate in raising her children by enjoying the bleeps and missteps of parenting along the way.

*You are not perfect. You are going to make mistakes. Just make sure, you enjoy the journey and fun of parenting. Be in the moment. Notice the dancer within each child, the uniqueness in seeing **your** child from a different perspective!*

Hugs from the Heart...

*When I am at
the end of my existence
on this earth,
when I am
"almost dead —
all wrinkly and
using a walking thing,"
I hope I still
have stories to tell...*

Storytelling by Grand-Moms & Moms

The Treasure that Remains

"Life can only be understood backwards; but it must be lived forwards." Soren Kierkegaard

By Marybeth from Florida

I am a storyteller. I love hearing, reading, and writing *our* stories. I say 'our' because there is *only one story*; we tell it over and over. It is the story of being human, and now that I am a grandmother, I treasure the nuggets provided by my darlings just as I do the stories shared with me when I was young.

Snuggled comfortably in the crook of my right arm is my six-year-old granddaughter. We are reading. Suddenly, she pulls away, turns my face away from the page and says: "Nana, I'm glad you're not dead yet."

I pull her in close, smile, look into her sweet, young face, and respond, "Oh yeah? Me too." My daughter tells me later that day that Brook's affirmation of my existence is likely related to the recent deaths of two great-grandparents on her father's side. Death concerns her. Death does not, however, seem to concern Brook's younger sister.

Norah decided at the age of four to become 'a baby doctor.' Good choice, as she would not be welcomed into a practice in geriatrics. Upon hearing the word 'ancestor' for the first time, she requested a definition from her mother, who explained that ancestors are people in our family who lived before us.

"Like Great-Grandma?" she questioned.

My daughter explained that the term is generally used to refer to family members who have died. Norah's matter of fact response was, "Well, she's almost dead. She's all wrinkly and uses that walking thing." We pray God gives her a more compassionate bedside manner.

When I was the age of my granddaughters, I loved when my grandmother and great-aunt came to visit. Yes, Norah, they are officially your ancestors as they are dead. Their visits generally occurred when my mother had just given birth to her latest child. As the oldest in my big, Irish-

Catholic family, I enjoyed frequent visits from these beloved women. My bedroom was the one with an extra bed, and I delighted in hearing tales from 'the olden days' as I lay in the dark, asking questions I hoped they would answer.

Being an ardent reader and film buff, I was obsessed, one summer, with 'The Roaring Twenties.' Knowing my great-aunt grew up in Chicago during this time period, I assumed she would share lurid details related to Prohibition and its consequences.

At first, she said her everyday life was quite ordinary. She worked as a secretary for the family business. Then, after much cajoling on my part, and likely a desire for sleep on hers, she said: "I do remember a time Marie and I were crossing the street downtown one day after work when we heard gunshots that stopped us in our tracks." Enthralled, I demanded more details—*gangsters? Frank Nitti?* Barrels of whiskey rolling out from trucks that were supposedly delivering oranges?

She snickered in response to my imagination, and in her no-holds-barred vernacular, stated:

"Cripes Murphy! We were scared to death. If shit were Shinola, our shoes would be polished."

Though my grandchildren often like to be 'scared to death' (at least some of them enjoy my 'scary' stories), I have not yet shared all my own adventures and those of grandmothers and great-aunts. Perhaps there will be a day when I relate how, as a young child, Great-Aunt Rita would cry and cry when her mother cautioned her to refrain from responding to a situation with an overabundance of 'drama.' When told: "Stop it, now; you'll die the death of an actress," the distraught child cried even more intensely, as she thought her mother was saying, "You'll die the death of a mattress." She had witnessed mattresses contaminated by illness thrown into the alley and set on fire—a routine practice in the early 1900's to deter contamination, a story that even the usually unaffected Norah might react to with empathy.

I cannot end my reverie without sharing my favorite memory of Great-Aunt Marie. If she had believed she was in danger of death on that Chicago street with her sister long ago, she never seemed concerned about the 'death' of her reputation as related to flatulence. Marie played the piano with passion, rolling out raucous tunes as if there was no tomorrow. Gathering around the piano after dinner was a common pastime, and having just finished a big meal, she thought nothing of lifting her ample derriere off the piano bench to emit a loud fart. "Better to bear the shame than bear the pain," she would say, and just keep on playing.

When I am at the end of my existence on this earth, when I am "almost dead—all wrinkly and using a walking thing," I hope I still have stories to tell and that those stories will be passed down for generations by those who have heard them. After all, they are 'our' stories.

Hugs from the Heart...

*More complicated
than what?
A gift of a car seat
without the gift
of installation
and instruction...
is no gift at all!*

Car Seats – The Best Gift Grandparents Can Receive!

"To become a grandparent is to enjoy one of the few pleasures in life for which the consequences have already been paid!"
Robert Breault

So, I am finally up in New England, and I'm anxious to see my baby grandkids! My husband and I enjoy our role as the new-generation grandparents. You know, the ones who spend part of their time here, and part there—often referred to as *Snow Birds* in Florida. I resent that title, though. I like to think of us as being able to spend loads of time with the grandkids up north and then with the two grandkids down south! I like to think of us as *Jet-Setting Grandparents!*

But the one thing I always seem to forget or ignore, is the car seat problem. So, adult children, here is a great gift for the grandparents who live in two locations, twice a year! Buy two car seats for the up-north times, and two car seats for the *"I'm going to visit, so I know there won't be car seats in Florida, or North Carolina, or wherever the grandparents are"* times. First, I'm assuming you may have two small children since you are older parents and want to have all your children before the pre-determined age of 40 or 35, or whatever the designated year of child completion is. Your babies are precious cargo, so help your aging parents out, for goodness sake!

Did you ever look at the car seat aisle in Walmart or Target or *any* baby store? There is no way ordinary grandparents—with Ph.D.'s even—can figure out, what all those car seats can do. They're large enough to place an engine on and take off by themselves. They're padded for safety. Translated: They add 50 more pounds to their original weight! The straps to push and pull baby are impossible to figure out, let alone install by one half-way intelligent grandparent. And there remains the daunting task of trying to figure out, which car seat the adult child or the grandparent can afford, with car seat costs varying upwards of $150.00. And then multiply that number by two! Plus tax!

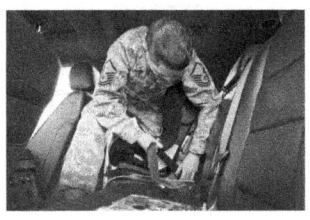

I went car seat shopping myself and can't figure out which one was suitable for which weight. How much does my grandchild weigh—now? And I need the height and age of the child too! *Before* I can determine which car seat to buy! And what about the padding? Is all that padding really necessary? And am I supposed to purchase a rear-facing car seat—and for which grandkid? The rules vary in every state! And how soon will they outgrow the rear-facing seat? Is it when their legs permanently turn into a pretzel because they have grown much too quickly, but still, according to the laws of that state, must stay facing backward? And when do they outgrow their new front-facing booster-seat? Is it when they kick the s**t out of the person in the front seat? And how much time must a grandparent spend in the local gym to gain enough upper body strength to hoist the rear-facing car seat with the baby which weighs a gazillion pounds, from the car to the stroller and then back into the correct 'thing-a-ma-jig,' so that the baby's car seat 'clicks' correctly into the socket and the baby is back securely strapped into the rear-facing car seat?

Give me a break! Parents can help navigate this tricky process, by giving grandparents the gift of a state-of-the-art car seat(s) as a Christmas gift, birthday gift, Mother's or Father's day gift. It would be much appreciated. *AND* also, while they are at it, give the precious gift of instruction. Even with my doctorate, or Dad's doctorate, neither one of us can figure out how to install the damn car seat. Cross my heart. I tried.

Two years ago, I had to go to the fire station and wait my turn, so that the twenty-something firefighter could install the new car seat. **But** since it wasn't the *'bring your car seat to the fire station and we'll install it'* day, the twenty-something firefighter with a young baby himself didn't have a clue about how to install it. He had last year's model. The car seats are more complicated now. **More complicated than what?** Nothing is more complicated than the installation of car seats, so a gift of a car seat of the parent's choice without the gift of installation and instruction (just in case in the off-chance the grandparent must pull the car seat out to use the seat for company), is no gift at all!

Adult children, please... realize, that the grandparents of the twenty-first century, while hip and 'with-it' in some respects, are no match for today's complicated car seats. Make sure, that if you want the grandparents to help with the grandkids, that good car seats, properly bought for the correct age and stage of your child's development **AND** properly installed by the parents, are the best investments a parent can make, and the kindest gift a grandparent can receive!

Hugs from the Heart...

*Our children
seem to understand
that the things we do —
and that we don't do —
are for a reason.*

Storytelling by Grand-Moms & Moms

Parenting is NOT a 'Judgment-Free Zone'

"Everything depends upon upbringing." Leo Tolstoy

By Aimee from Massachusetts

Ooooof! I watch as my 10-year-old daughter, Abby, is tackled to the floor in the middle of the public library. She and her 'assailant,' 6-year-old Danny, both roll to their feet, dust themselves off, and smile at each other. One of my dearest friends, Danny's Mom, bends down to speak directly with Danny. "When we see a friend we say *hi* and give a hug, not knock them down."

Danny just finished kindergarten, and as a child on the autism spectrum, he's still working out his social queues. His Mom has often told me she wishes she had a shirt she could put on him when they're out places that says something like, "Pardon me, I have Autism…"—because, unlike some other developmental issues that have visible signs, children on the autism spectrum can sometimes look like they're just children who are terribly behaved, and that their parents can't control them.

It's Danny's Mom's fear of the judgment of others around her, as well as a number of experiences I've had with my own two rambunctious darlings, that made me really take notice: Parenting is *NOT* a 'judgment-free zone.'

At the start of this great adventure in parenting, my husband and I had a number of lengthy discussions about how we saw the whole process of parenting, knowing that there would need to be some flexibility for the specific needs of our children. We talked about our own childhoods, what we thought looking back had worked well— *or not*. We also talked about our general philosophies about raising children.

We came up with some guidelines that we wanted to make sure we kept in mind, when we had children ourselves. I can tell you – it was nothing earth-shattering or extreme. We felt strongly, that we needed structure. We would be a family of two working parents. Structure and routine would be necessary for all of us, especially since we were definitely *Type-A* personalities! For example, the children would need to have a set bedtime, so we could have time to talk and spend together after the children were asleep, as well as to do chores that we couldn't get done with them underfoot. We felt incredibly strong about the importance of responsibility and accountability, making sure those were things we could both model and teach the children.

It's hard to explain to a child that there's a big difference between, "I'm sorry I broke that; it was an accident." *and* "I didn't mean to." One acknowledges that you had a role in whatever went wrong and conveys remorse. The other tries to negate the outcome based on a lack of intent. While difficult, these are concepts we continue to find critical to share with the children as they get older.

Then there was the big one: discipline. I found that particularly when the children were small, there needed to be an immediacy to disciplining the children that was sometimes uncomfortable. I couldn't go back to a two-year-old, hours after he has had a total melt-down at the store, and explain to him, that his behavior, before nap time, was unacceptable, and that *now* he was getting a time-out. That never works!

So, I got very comfortable with the concept of disciplining the children in front of people. They never seemed to care that they were being complete terrors, and embarrassing me in front of people. Why should I be bothered dealing with their behavior in front of the people that had just seen it? I walked out of stores with screaming children. I didn't give in—even if it were a choice between a $3.00 junk toy or a total meltdown—*bring it on!*

I'm not buying compliance. I kept telling myself that being consistent and making the right choices was the right way to go. *Except* there was just one issue—Parenting is NOT a judgment-free zone.

I was ready for the comments: "I think you're psychologically damaging your children."

Excuse me! What the heck did you just say?

It was a Friday night after a long week at work. Aren't all weeks at work long ones? My two children, husband, and I were over at the neighbors for pizza and a few adult beverages, with juice boxes for the little people. At dinner, the neighbor's 6-year-old, Molly, climbed up *onto* the kitchen table and stood in the center of the table while all the other children kept on eating their pizza and looking at her pink shoes.

No one said anything. Her parents showed little interest in disciplining her to get down from the table. I could see my husband physically restraining himself from grabbing her and putting her on the floor. After dinner, Nate, my son, was acting rowdy. I raised my voice—moderately—to get his attention. I let him know that his behavior was totally unacceptable, and that if he didn't stop, I would take him home. Everything seemed to settle down, so the adults went to a different room to get a little quiet time from the kiddos.

Boom! That was when my neighbor dropped her judgment on me!

Now, in the interest of full disclosure—I know that I'm loud. *And* I'm loud when I don't even know I'm being loud, if that makes any sense. So, to me, raising my voice moderately, may have sounded like I was screaming bloody murder. But I didn't think so.

Either way, I hadn't made any remarks when Molly was standing six inches from Nate's steaming slice of pizza—*on the kitchen table*. My friend told me what she thought: "When you raise your voice, I think you're psychologically damaging your children." I wrapped up the evening as quickly as possible and left!

I was devastated. This was judgment from someone that I considered a close friend, and who knew our family well? I certainly could have made things much easier on ourselves by adopting a *'whatever'* attitude with our children, but taking the easy way out wasn't what we wanted. I didn't want to raise children that thought acting inappropriately (crazy) in public was okay, *or* that making poor decisions didn't have consequences.

I'd always considered that these neighbors had a very different parenting style than we did, but just assumed that they did what worked for them. And while their 'style' of discipline for their children was occasionally annoying, when we would spend time together, I never would have considered passing judgment on them because of it. We understand that the way we do things wouldn't work for everyone, just the way other people manage their family dynamics wouldn't work for us.

My children are bright, considerate, inquisitive and well-spoken. They are comfortable with their spot in the world and by all accounts are well-adjusted. I don't feel the need to justify the choices I make for them as their Mom to anyone; but in that moment, visiting our friends, I felt the full weight of the judgment they passed on the parenting choices we make.

As the children have gotten older—Abby is 10 years old now, and Nate is 8 years old—they have started asking questions about some of the differences they see in the way things happen at our house vs. their friends' houses.

One night last summer, I was tucking Nate into bed, and he could see his neighborhood friends outside, still riding bikes. He asked why *he* had to go to bed and why *they* didn't. I was honest with him, "There are a couple of reasons: 1. They don't go to camp, so they can sleep later tomorrow. 2. People need different amounts of sleep. Nate, you sleep from 8:30 at night until 8:00 in the morning, almost EVERY night. Your bike-riding friend is up by 5:45 AM daily without an alarm."

The good news is, once I explained this honestly to him, he was happy to go to sleep. The children ask why some people eat out more than we do. I told them, "Mom likes to cook so we are able to eat dinner together and talk about our day, at home, where it's quiet, and we can hear each other."

They ask why some friends do travel sports and they don't. I'm always honest with them, even if the answer is that Mom and Dad just can't handle the time commitment for travel sports. Our children seem to understand that the things we do—and that we don't do—are for a reason. Now that they're old enough to understand, we're happy to share the reasons with them. They're not always thrilled, but they understand.

As new challenges come up, we talk about them. When our neighbors and we became friends, at the beginning, it was because her daughter was friends with Abby. As a family, we had a conversation with the children about Danny. They were too little to understand the idea of 'Autism'. Autism is such a varied disorder and is manifested so differently from child to child, it really wouldn't have helped to try to explain it. So, we talked about the idea that Danny learned a little differently, and sometimes might not understand how to act in certain situations. But Danny is our friend, and we include him in our activities and treat him with kindness and respect.

We had the same discussion when a new family with a child with Down syndrome moved to our neighborhood. Wouldn't the world be a better place if Danny's mom could take Danny anywhere she wanted without worrying about people reacting poorly if he gets overstimulated by a noisy situation? If, as parents, we felt supported in our decisions, even if they weren't the same as others were making?

I'm sure almost every parent has a story like mine. Hopefully not as extreme, but a moment that you were somewhere with your children and felt like someone was passing judgment on you. Next time you see a frazzled Mom at *Target* with

Hugs from the Heart...

a screaming toddler, maybe instead of just walking by, ask her if she needs any help. It's more productive to pass on *kindness* than judgment!

Hugs from the Heart...

*What has happened
to this Dad,
who looks like a
highly intelligent human being,
and one who is probably
in charge of
a dozen people at work?
Why — to our surprise —
he's a flaming idiot!*

Remember that Dads are Parents Too!

"The heart of a father is the masterpiece of nature."
Antoine Francois Prevost d'Exiles

Father's Day is every June, and I'm thinking that maybe this Father's Day, they will finally get the recognition they deserve. Every Father's Day it seems, I open up the newspaper to headlines buried deep into the middle of the paper which read: *"Deadbeat Dads ..."*—you fill in the blank. Wouldn't it be just the best Dad's day present for our newspapers to actually *Celebrate Father-*

hood instead of bash it with a baseball bat? There must be something good we can say about Dads besides their contribution of sperm.

    I, as the mother of two adult sons, weep for a world where we value our fathers so little, that we place commercials on television about Dads who can't take care of their children without Moms around. Remember the recent commercial—I know you've seen it—where the father and his children are *Facetiming* Mom, who is on a business trip and eagerly awaiting a good visual of her family before she goes to sleep after a long business day. She is tentative about how Dad is handling the family, but fortunately for her, Dad puts on a good show. The children assure her that 'everything's good' at home. Dad assures her' that he has everything under control too. I

don't think she buys it, though. However, she doesn't say anything out loud. Thank God! The kids look clean and presentable.

Is it so absurd to believe that all is well on the home-front and that Dad can, in fact, handle three kids and one toddler? Come on! We, the audience doubt Dad's capabilities from the start of this commercial. It's like we are waiting for the punchline. And we get it soon after Mom hangs up! The camera pans over the kitchen, where food is stuck to every square inch of the walls and the entire kitchen is upside down. What has happened to this Dad, who looks like a highly intelligent human being, and one who is probably in charge of a dozen people at work? Why—*to our surprise*—he's a flaming idiot! He can't control his children's behavior when Mom's out of town. At the end, he is seen scrubbing the walls getting the crud off, before Mom gets home the next day, 'cause that's how long this mess will take to clean up!

Now, if this were an isolated commercial on television, I'd be shocked. But this type of mentality of a father's ability to participate in raising a family should have all men up in arms. Why are men barnstormers in their own careers, but not able to organize, to protest their treatment of being viewed as incompetent fathers in the real world. You probably know many, many instances where poor, old Dad gets the short end of the stick! Men, rise up! Show the world you will not take this visual abuse on television, in newspapers, or anywhere else.

I know you can change a diaper without getting all queasy and passing out! *I know* you can feed a baby without getting spaghetti stuck to the walls! *I know* you can give Jr. a bath without drowning the kid! You need to tell the rest of the world that you are the rule, not the exception. It shouldn't be so shocking to see a man and his children out to breakfast or dinner without saying that this must be 'Wednesday' or the every-other-weekend that Dad gets the kids. Most people assume that fathers seen out and about with their own children are divorced! Maybe they just plain want to take their kids out to have some father/child quality time. My sons are amazing fathers who actively *and* productively *and* wholeheartedly participate in their children's lives. There are many millions more like them.

Take charge of your fatherhood! Write or email or *tweet* out to the world that you are the 'real deal.' That you won't be the brunt of this *'incompetent, idiot Dad'* culture we have created in this country. It's at a point where we don't even realize how poorly we are treating Dads.

Let all of us protest the stereotyping of Dads everywhere. Let's be aware of it and do something about it.

Let's stop treating Dad's like they are outsiders looking into the family and let's treat them as if they are a vital part of family. Let's not give lip service to fathers this year, but rather give thanks for Dad's contributions as the heart of the family.

Hugs from the Heart...

*She knew
she was facing her own struggle
to communicate with the children.
She gets it!
I think children teach us.*

Children Teach Us!

"While we try to teach our children all about life, our children teach us what life is all about." Angela Schwindt

By Paulette from Iowa

Nothing is as heart-wrenching as seeing a child crying, whether from fear, or from feelings that have been assaulted. The tears are real and touch my soul.

Today was a typical day. We had our usual discussion on what we wanted to wear, and Quinn focused on thinking about which selection of shirt and shorts she wanted to wear. Her busy mind decided on color, and socks, and shoes. To me it's teaching life's lessons, giving her a sense of independence and accomplishment, even to such seemingly simple tasks. My granddaughter is autistic, so the small victories are savored.

Today we chose a flowered shirt and pink shorts. We sat down for a bit and then decided what adventure we would try today.

First on the agenda was music. That's always a favorite. We danced and laughed and sang. Then we decided to go to the 'Park,' which really was the school playground, the one she will be attending when she starts school next year. They just added a merry-go-round. Lovely! But a grandmother has to have the strength of Hercules to turn it. And plenty of oomph to run in circles chasing after it! It's exhausting to have to turn the handles on top or sit and push with your feet, neither of which I am currently capable of! Thank goodness there were others there, much younger, to do the manual labor: two children, a boy and girl, their parents, and a social worker.

The children and parents wandered off to the basketball court. Then I noticed Quinn, my granddaughter, hiding under the suspension bridge. She was crying. The tears streamed down her face. It was if razors tore into me. "What's wrong," I asked, really knowing the answer before I even asked the question.

"Play ball! Me play ball." She was hurt because the children left and didn't ask her to play with them.

I said, "Let's go ask."

Apparently, because she does not speak clearly, and sometimes just *signs* instead, the children thought she was ignoring them. I explained the situation to the children, and she was asked to join in and play.

This has me a bit scared for her. I did try to explain to Quinn why the children misunderstood her. In order to explain it to Quinn clearly, I drew a square with a flower inside. I then asked her what I drew. She immediately said flower.

I said, "Yes! There is a flower, but the flower is in a square. Sometimes we see things differently. The kids only saw the flower, too. You have to look at the whole picture—everything—to understand. They weren't trying to hurt your feelings. They just didn't understand."

I think, or, at least I hope, it helped her. When we got home she ran to the fridge. I post pictures on the fridge. Quinn then began naming everything on the fridge magnets, plus on the cards and notes.

I think Quinn is focusing on the challenge before her—*trying to find the right words.* How do I explain the meaning of this experience to a five year old? And other verbal challenges she may face? She seemed to 'get it' at the playground today. She knew she was facing her own struggle to communicate with the children. *She gets it!* I think children teach us. Quinn certainly taught me how to overcome the challenge of language today. More than I taught her.

Storytelling by Grand-Moms & Moms

Hugs from the Heart...

*Your child
is the lovely smoothie
that you created.
Now he's about to explode,
but not because
of anything you did.*

Storytelling by Grand-Moms & Moms

A Two-Year-Old is like a Blender without a Lid!

"A two-year-old is kind of like having a blender, but you don't have a top for it." Jerry Seinfeld

Did you ever try to make a smoothie? Should be simple, right? Just pile in the veggies or the fruit, add ice cubes, maybe water or almond milk, or whatever? Mix it up on high, or low if you want to see the ingredients fold into the mix, and voilà! A lovely drink, smooth, no trace of any one thing, but a delicious and creamy combination that pleases the pallet. *BUT*, mix the ingredients without the lid on, and the whole thing explodes all over the place!.

Well, it's like that with two-year-olds! If you're a first-time Mom, you look forward to a child's growth—intellectually, emotionally, and physically! After all, you positively measure everything every day and chart your baby's growth. You have all the books on what to expect at each stage of your child's growth and development. It seems almost too neat and precise. Ask any seasoned Mom! The book *says*... and so you measure as told by the latest 'expert' of the day! Now everybody with a Ph.D. has a book out!

The experts are pretty generic in their expectations. You long for the Two Year Old stage. You know intellectually, that Baby is small and helpless, and it is your duty as a parent to teach, to parent, to nanny, *to... to... to....* *But if your child were only two years old*, at least he could walk by himself, climb up on the couch by himself, climb up into the car seat by himself, and—

bonus—you might actually get the needed rest your weary body deserves!

Did you actually think that would really happen? Didn't you see the word *terrible* before the word *twos*? They do it purposely you know—to stay vague. *Terrible* is a vague and really huge word that experts hope you will gloss over. Actually, you ask yourself, how terrible can that really be, after all? You've been through child birth, through breast-feeding 24/7, through almost two years of sleep deprivation, through intimacy issues with your significant other because Baby is sleeping smack dab between the two of you most of the time, even though Baby has a designer crib to sleep in—with mobiles hanging from the sky and toys that entertain him, should he awaken, and sound vibrations that should, theoretically, lull him to sleep instantaneously! But that never works.

Your child is the lovely smoothie that you created. Now he's about to explode, but not because of anything you did. Everything you've ever known about this little, predictable bundle of joy, is about to change. Your way of life will be changed forever. Just when you have his nap schedule down pat, so that you do have an extra minute to clean, or read, or do work on your computer (you can usually set your clock by his nap-time routine), all hell breaks loose—hence the *Terrible Twos* wreak havoc on every aspect of your life. The lid is off the blender and the s**t has hit the fan!

No more predictable schedule! Your child lives in the moment, literally. If he feels like toddling over to the dog and pulling his tail, or opening the lock on a doorknob advertised as 'child proof,' or toddling over to visit your neighbors, without asking permission—he will do just that! He might stop several times, to pick grass, or watch a pigeon s**t on your car, or jump into a puddle! He may take off his shoes and hurl them at passing cars, or even sit down on the sidewalk to watch ants walk by. That's two. He's never where you think he is.

Learning consumes every waking moment—*the good, the bad, and the ugly*. He is sensory, all taste buds on high alert as he picks through the garbage, or unwraps a poopy diaper and places it on his head, poop and all—trust me, true story! You can't make that stuff up! He is tactile. He feels the texture of food, learning about cause and effect, as he tosses his squished spaghetti on the floor or mashes it into his hair. He's in the moment, and you can smile if you realize this phenomenon! No iPad or fancy toys needed. In the moment. No interactive anything required.

He is the interloper, the one who makes things happen. He learns through bodily movements what happens to him if he runs too fast—and then cries for *you* when he runs into the proverbial wall, because his center of gravity has not yet matured and he just can't stop in time!

He's really in the *Terrific Twos*, *if* you can see the learning take place and participate when asked, or when he is about to electrocute himself by experimenting. For instance, what happens to a fork when he sticks it into the electrical socket? You know, but he's bound and determined to find out for himself. Oh, you thought those child proof caps would hang tight to the plugs? You really thought they would protect Baby from a electrocuting himself? Silly you! A two-year-old can figure out things a rocket scientist could only dream about!

Oh, did I forget to tell you that a two-year-old is opinionated and bossy and loves the word *NO*, even if he doesn't mean no, but really means *YES!* It makes him feel powerful. He *must* feel he is in control. And he throws the temper tantrum to prove it! His demanding nature, if channeled, can turn him into tomorrow's leader! You might provide some choice, limiting him a choice between two things. And allow your toddler to figure out which one suits him best! Then later, add one more choice to the mix. Remember, the lid is off. All bets are off, unless you find the lid—translated—reign in the choices. But do give some responsibility to your toddler. Never take the lid entirely off! Never say, "What do you want to do?" Too broad, no control, and a major mistake! If your little tyke wants to take a trip to grandma's house and she lives in Alaska, that's out! So limit the scope of choices to things you know are possible.

And always remember that your toddler is constantly thinking outside the neat little box your books on stages of growth and development have placed him in. Be prepared for him to feed the cat your bake-sale cookies or place a large creative mural on your freshly painted living room wall—and you thought you were watching his every movement! You don't have eyes in the back of your head. It only takes a nanosecond for creativity or danger to rear its ugly head, and for chaos to reign down on your smoothly run house.

Your child needs creative outlets, true. Allowing a 'free zone'—like the driveway and chalk, or a place he can let it all hang out, will pay dividends. Who knows, he may to the next Picasso—and your patience will not be worn thin.

Hang tight! And don't rush the *Terrible Twos*. Savor them, knowing that soon, your child will be a parent himself, and your memories will be captured on your photo-frame, endlessly rolling round and round on your bureau, reminding you of the good old days.

Remember to keep the blender whirring along,

with the lid sometimes half on, but never entirely off. Let this amazing two-year-old mix up his own smoothie, his own creative way of experiencing the world. Your job is to guide him, to watch, and laugh, as he makes sense out of everything! Be in the moment with your toddler.

I'm not even going to tell you what to expect when your child is a teenager! That's too scary a thought!

Hugs from the Heart

*I close my eyes,
and I see your face,
small, round, untouched by time,
gazing up into mine.*

*I linger in the moment,
hovering between what is and what was…*

*I count the days,
until childhood ends and something else begins,
when endless hugs are no longer
spontaneously given
for every occasion... or just because...*

*I treasure this memory of hugs and kisses,
one more time,
since I can only bring myself to count to ten…
and the time flies by, and years beyond…*

*Before…the circle of life begins anew
and you have babies of your own,
I have only you,
at this moment of eyes wide shut.*

*Until… I think of my grandchild,
and the cycle of life
I gaze into my grandchild's eyes
… again, as with you,
        … Hugs from the Heart…*

                          Margaret M. Desjardins

Contributors

Paulette Buco

Paulette Buco was born in New England and is currently living in Iowa. She is the mother of three, grandmother of eleven, and great-grandmother of two. Her work and children have given her the opportunity to live in several states, resulting in great adventures that have become stories from the heart. Her greatest joy is seeing the future in the eyes of children.

Tricia Murphy Duffy

Tricia Murphy Duffy is a Jersey girl who moved to SW Florida 38 years ago with her husband, Barney. She has spent most of her career in healthcare management, marketing and recently retired as a Charlotte County Commissioner. She and Barney have three children and three young grandchildren.

Hugs from the Heart...

Jan McGregor

Jan McGregor is a retired elementary school teacher who enjoys spending time with her husband, Ron. She also loves babysitting her grandchildren and volunteering in her granddaughter's first grade classroom. When time permits, she and her husband like to search for waterfalls in the Carolinas.

Amy Ruocco

Amy Ruocco is the mother of two, a children's support advocate and a fierce warrior for dyslexic children. Through her website MamabearMoms.com, she educates parents about the importance of early identification of dyslexia and teaches them how to advocate for appropriate interventions.

Lydia Rutter

Since retiring after 35 years with a local school system in south Florida, Lydia Rutter spends as much time as she can with family, especially her three great-grandchildren. She also enjoys swimming, baking, and helping out neighbors and friends as needed. And, oh yes, she spoils her husband with her wonderful cooking.

Aimee Sawyer

Aimee Sawyer is a mom of two, and in her endless quest to be mother of the year can often be found baking, doing craft projects or helping with homework—to be followed by copious amounts of wine or occasional raised voices. She loves traveling with her family and sharing new experiences with her little people. In her 'spare time' she works for a Fortune 100 Financial Services Company.

Kate Sharp

Kate is an American expat that now calls bonny Scotland home. She enjoys traveling the world, live music, and gym life. Always with her game face on, the accidental SAHM mom of three relies on humor, strong coffee, lots of prosecco, and her tribe of fierce friends as she navigates this whole adulting phase.

Marybeth Vaughan

Marybeth Vaughan, who wrote her first story at age seven, has also been acting, singing and dancing all her life. She thanks God daily for making her an artist and, at seventy, for the ability to evoke laughter from her seven kids and nine grandkids. "What, Nana? You're learning Chinese Dance?" She is; artists are artists forever.

Karen Yohe

Karen Yohe was born in NY and currently resides in Florida. She has two children but feels as if she really has four. Karen has held many jobs but her longest stint was as a college math instructor; she now is a full-time stay-at-home mom. She enjoys cooking because she likes to eat, and reading because she can.

Christine Zimmer

Christine Zimmer, a retired educator, is the mother of two and grandmother of four. She loves spending time with her nuclear and extended family members and friends, volunteering with church and non-profit children's organizations, bonsai gardening, reading. and traveling. Her writing is mostly confined to grants at this time, but who knows what the future may bring!

Dr. Margaret M. Desjardins has been an elementary and middle school teacher, a school administrator, and a reading consultant. Most recently, she has been a professor of English and creative writing at Florida SouthWestern State College. With three children and nine grandchildren scattered about the globe, all with distinctive personalities, she has plenty of stories to tell. She lives in Punta Gorda, Florida, with her husband, Rene, and two fun-loving dogs, Max and Oliver, for six months of the year, and on an island in New England close to Boston for the other half of the year.

Other Books by Margaret M. Desjardins

Touching the Soul...
Connecting through Poetry

Margaret's Illustrated Book Series for Children
Suggested for readers in grades K-3

Murky, Quirky, Beserky Math
Simon and his friends learn to have fun with Math in Mrs. Smith's class!

No Time for Dinosaurs
Simon and his friends miss learning about dinosaurs in Mrs. Smith's class...

The Trouble with the Dungeon
(with Isabella Desjardins)

Isabella must find her courage to fight off dragons and witches on her way to a dungeon deep under a castle.

The Rainbow Kitty Series

Suggested for readers in grades K-3

Shannon O'Bean Saves the Tooth Fairy

The leprechaun began chasing the Tooth Fairy.
Could the little green kitty come to the rescue?

Paddipaws Saves the Friendship

Just what would become of this little kitty? Would he remember to use his magic tail?

Mr. Biggles Saves the Best Teacher Ever

Timothy's regular teacher had disappeared. His substitute teacher was mean. What now?

Flibberty-Jibberty Saves the Sleepover

Julia would run away from her mean sisters. Will Flibberty-Jibberty use his magic tail to help her?

Pumpkin-Puss Saves the Birthday

Pumpkin-Puss was an itsy bitsy kitty and her entire body was stuck in a large green bottle. Things would only get worse.

Stinky Pete Saves the Camping Trip

Stinky Pete had polka-dots hopping all over his body and he was giving off his stinky odor. Could he still become friends with Edward?

Zoe-Zoe Saves the School Play

Will Zoe-Zoe use her magic tail to grant Maeven's wish? Will Zoe-Zoe ever see her family again?

The Z-Dawg Series
Suggested for readers in grades 4-9

The Haunting of Swallow Cave
This haunting tale of mystery and intrigue twists and turns, as two modern-day teenage cousins untangle a 340-year-old island mystery.

The Pirate Ghost of Dungeon Cave
Zack finds himself in *attack* mode, as he and his friends search deep into the *Lynn Woods Reservation* at midnight to solve the mystery of the pirate and the lost treasure.

The Screaming Witch of Olde Salem Village
Zack and his Grandpa are living in a haunted apartment building high on a hill, in a place that was once *Ground Zero* for the witch trials held in 1692. Evil resides.

The Specter of the Black Cat
When Zack finds a note in an old box in Bean's attic, written by Bean's ancestor admitting to murder and plundering a ship for gold during the Civil War, Zack knows their lives are in danger.

Purchase this book and other books listed here
through my Facebook Page, Margaret's Views:
https://www.facebook.com/margaretsviews,
where you can review the many other interesting posts and visit
the Shop Page. Locate the menu on the left side of the main page,
then click on the word Shop to order and receive your discount.
Discount only available when ordering directly
through my Facebook Page.

www.ingramcontent.com/pod-product-compliance
Lightning Source LLC
Chambersburg PA
CBHW061428040426
42450CB00007B/945